英美名詩一百首
100 GREAT ENGLISH POEMS

一百叢書

英漢對照 English-Chinese

孫梁編選

英美名詩一百首
100 GREAT ENGLISH POEMS

商務印書館

叢書編輯：羅　斯
執行編輯：曾振邦
設　　計：溫一沙

《一百叢書》
英美名詩一百首
100 GREAT ENGLISH POEMS
孫梁編選

出版：商務印書館（香港）有限公司
　　　香港鰂魚涌芬尼街2號D僑英大廈
印刷：美雅印刷製本有限公司
　　　九龍官塘榮業街6號海濱工業大廈4樓B1
版次：1986年5月第1版
　　　1995年3月第4次印刷
　　　© 1986 商務印書館（香港）有限公司
　　　ISBN 962 07 1064 9
　　　Printed in Hong Kong

《一百叢書》總序

　　本館出版英漢(或漢英)對照《一百叢書》的目的,是希望憑藉着英、漢兩種語言的對譯,把中國和世界各類著名作品的精華部分介紹給中外讀者。

　　本叢書的涉及面很廣。題材包括了寓言、詩歌、散文、短篇小說、書信、演說、語錄、神話故事、聖經故事、成語故事、名著選段等等。

　　顧名思義,《一百叢書》中的每一種都由一百個單元組成。以一百為單位,主要是讓編譯者在浩瀚的名著的海洋中作挑選時有一個取捨的最低和最高限額。至於取捨的標準,則是見仁見智,各有心得。

　　由於各種書中被選用的篇章節段,都是以原文或已被認定的範本作藍本,而譯文又經專家學者們精雕細琢,千錘百煉,故本叢書除可作為各種題材的精選讀本外,也是研習英漢兩種語言對譯的理想參考書,部分更可用作朗誦教材。外國學者如要研習漢語,本叢書亦不失為理想工具。

商務印書館(香港)有限公司
編輯部

前　　言

　　詩海無涯，本集所選滄海一粟而已。但編選的宗旨是明確的，即百花齊放，雅俗共賞。編者力圖選擇有代表性的、廣爲傳誦或具特色的作品。各種傾向與流派的詩人及其創作，無論其爲現實主義、古典主義、浪漫主義，象徵派或玄學派，激進的或保守的，以及不標榜什麼主義、不屬於任何流派者，都兼收並蓄。然而，舉凡無病呻吟的陳腔濫調、徒尙藻飾的駢詞儷句，以及御用文人歌功頌德的篇章（如騷賽應制之作，儘管其作品不盡屬此類），概不入選。

　　本編上起"英詩之父"（屈拉頓語）喬叟，下迄介乎傳統與現代派之間的愛德華·托馬斯。限於篇幅，實際上至近代末期爲止。

　　在主題和素材、內容和形式等方面不拘一格。觸景生情，感物言志，沉思冥想，感慨身世，滿腔孤憤等形形色色思想感情，在各種詩人筆下俱臻其妙。大至探索宇宙奧秘，探討人生意義，抒發愛國熱情；或爲反抗暴虐與侵略，爲爭取自由和解放而慷慨悲歌，或以嚴肅的態度詠述含有哲理及道德意味的情思；或者抒寫離愁，懷念故土。許多詩人以如椽之筆描繪大自然壯麗同秀美的景色，情景交融。亦有不少詩人環繞生與死、愛與憎等"永恒的主題"而低徊詠嘆，或抒唱愛情的甘苦(bitter-sweet，古希臘女詩人莎孚語)，情文並茂。有些詩則如爐邊絮談，敘家常瑣事而傾訴純樸的感情（如柯珀作《我的瑪麗》）。

由於本集中傳統詩居多，故而大都格律謹嚴，講究音韵和遣詞煉句，也有節奏自然的自由詩。然而，無論遵守格律或自由發揮，詩人們往往靈活地運用明喻或隱喻、轉喻或逆喻，象徵和意象，聯想與暗示，以及排比、對照、反襯、偶句和雙關語等技巧。有些詩人寫得樸素自然，明白如話，或用對話與獨白等方式。種種手法都用來表達或寄托詩人的情懷與哲思，或寫景狀物，創造獨特的意境，或直抒性靈而耐人尋味。

至於譯者也是"各顯神通"。從我國新詩的奠基者郭沫若與聞一多開始，爾後是五四運動前後接踵而起的詩人朱湘、卞之琳、周煦良和梁宗岱等。此外有當代研究和翻譯詩歌的專家學者方重、王佐良、袁可嘉、查良錚（筆名穆旦）、趙蘿蕤、徐遲、方平、豐華瞻、朱維之、殷寶書、楊德豫、荒蕪、蘇仲翔等。並有素養頗深的中年教師及譯者，以至青年學者。迻譯的風格多種多樣。有些譯者力求忠實於原作，恪守原詩格律；另一些譯者側重於曲傳神韵,"統攝原意,另鑄新辭"(郭沫若語)[1]。亦有介乎其間者。某些譯者用舊詩詞體,或帶有舊詩風味;皆備一格,以供參照。譯詩自然以新詩爲主,但有些外國詩以舊詩詞格調迻譯,似乎詩味較濃些。總之,從前輩詩人的譯品以至當代的譯詩來看,不僅顯示了絢爛多姿的風格,而且多少反映了近代至現代我國詩歌翻譯的發展。

選本不同於評論,不宜憑主觀傾向"宗唐"或"佞宋",崇古典而斥浪漫,或反之。譬如畫廊,應陳列各派藝術品,供趣味別的觀衆鑒賞。誠然,某些選本還是有傾向性的,如張惠言所輯《詞選》,在自序中開宗明義地闡述《說文》釋義:"意內而言外謂之詞;"並據此而主張"微言比興"之義,"幽約怨悱"之情,反對"雕琢曼辭",故選錄極嚴,不合此原則者,大都捨棄。精則精矣,恐略嫌偏頗耳。

又如以前的《牛津詩選》,根據正統觀點,貶低"離經叛道"的拜倫等詩人,對於他們的作品,選取較少。雖然在詩藝上,拜倫較粗疏,但就其詩歌總的內容與精神而言,無疑是上乘的,因而年長的歌德對這位青年詩人推崇備至,稱之爲"本世紀最大的有才能的詩人,"

---

[1] 見郭沫若《屈原賦今譯·九歌解題》。原指以新詩體譯楚辭,亦適用於郭譯外國詩歌。

"他可以比得上莎士比亞。"[1]至於憲章派詩人,如歐內斯特·瓊斯等,則上述詩選以及帕爾格雷夫選的《英詩萃編》(*The Golden Treasury*)乾脆擯棄了。然而,隨着歷史的進展,較新的選集似乎放寬些尺度,如五十年代的《企鵝詩選》、六十年代的《英語詩歌菁英》(奧斯卡·威廉斯編)[2],以及七十年代的《劍橋詩選》等,均不那麼保守了。

從本集所選四十多位英美詩人的作品,可以看出"江山代有才人出,各領風騷數百年。"(趙翼:《甌北詩話·論詩》)這些詩篇不僅反映了各派詩人的遞嬗、各種詩風的興替,並且傳達了不同時代的風貌與本質。因為詩不但是一個民族的語言中最精粹的部份,而且如麥修·阿諾德所云:"詩乃人心之精髓;詩人正視生活,並觀其全貌;所以要了解特定時代的精神,須從當時的詩歌中尋覓。"[3]

按詩的性質來講,不外乎"言志"(《尚書·堯典》)和"緣情"(陸機:《文賦》)兩大

---

(1) 見朱光潛譯《歌德談話錄》,頁65及150;人民文學出版社,1982年。

(2) Oscar Williams (ed.): *Master Poems of the English Language*。書內各篇詩歌後附有現代詩人學者所撰寫的評論,分析精細,見解獨到。

(3) 見麥修·阿諾德著《文藝評論集》(*Essays in Criticism*)。

類。其實不必截然區分。好詩大都兼而有之，所謂"在心為志，發言為詩；情動於中，而形於言。"（《詩大序》）或如劉勰所云："人稟七情，應物斯感，感物吟志，莫非自然。"（《文心雕龍·明詩篇》）(1) 這些話切中肯綮，總之，在詩歌中，情與志是統一或交融的；與其像陸機所說"詩緣情而綺靡"，不如說"詩緣情而言志"，並以情為主。

這情必須是真的，有真情實感才能扣人心弦。陶潛之所以格高千古，主要由於其襟懷"曠而且真"（昭明太子：《陶集序》）。近代詩人中，龔定庵的詩傳誦一時，因為他"歌泣無端字字真"（《己亥雜詩》）(2)。本集內許多詩都真情畢露。譬如所選蘇格蘭詩人彭斯的幾首，無論激昂慷慨地高歌愛國之情，或表達對被壓迫者誠摯的同情，或抒唱純潔的眷戀之情，莫不發自肺腑，感人至深。即使在詩中談哲理、發議論，也得有真知灼見；不過這類詩總覺乏味些，並非正道。

真摯的感情又須自然地表達，不堆砌詞藻，不矯揉造作，不掉書袋，不用晦澀的象徵

---

(1) 見范文瀾注《文心雕龍》上冊，頁65；人民文學出版社，1958年。
(2) 《龔自珍全集》，頁526；上海人民出版社，1975年。

和冷僻的隱喻,而是即景生情,直抒胸臆。在這一點上,鍾嶸講得透闢:"觀古今勝語,多非補假,皆由直尋。"(《詩品序》)(1)沃茲沃斯給詩下的定義有類似的意思:"詩乃強有力的情感自發地洋溢。"(Poetry is the spontaneous overflow of powerful feelings.)(2)所謂"直尋"和"自發"均爲天然之意。

因此,率眞與自然是編選本集時取捨的準則之一。這並不意味着入選的每一篇都體現這兩點,但這裏不少詩篇確實如此。僅舉數例,如沃茲沃斯幾首膾炙人口的短詩,蘭德的絕句《終曲》,以及阿倫·坡的名篇《安娜貝·李》,等等。儘管表達的思想感情不同,風格和技巧迥異;並且體裁不一,或抒情,或敍事,或蘊含哲思,或以悽婉的衷情悼念亡妻;但自然地流露眞情却是一致的。

文藝創作必須運用形象思維(也要通過邏輯思維),寫詩尤其如斯。所以,詩的特徵是以形象化手段,如我國歷來詩論中闡述的比興,西方文論中剖析的意象、象徵、隱喻和博喻等,加上排偶、對比、轉折與襯托等修辭法,構成精妙的意境;或如王靜安標舉的境界,其

---

(1) 《詩品注》,頁7;人民文學出版社,1958年。
(2) 見E. D. Jones編 *English Critical Essays: Nineteenth Century* (Oxford University Press, 1932),頁26。

中分"有我之境"與"無我之境"[1],即主觀地抒情或表明理想同客觀地寫景狀物之分,或兩者揉合。正如王氏所說:"二者(指理想與寫實)頗難分別,因大詩人所造之境必合乎自然,所寫之境亦必鄰於理想故也。"這些分析頗有見地。同時,詩的意境也常含有嚴羽倡言的"氣象"、"興趣"(類似情趣)和"韵味"("羚羊掛角,無迹可求"),以及王漁洋繼承嚴說而大暢其旨的"神韵"。[2]

上述特徵和境界在本集所選的詩篇中有不同程度的表現。例如納希作《春天》基本上描繪了含華敷榮的"無我之境"。葛雷的《鄉村墓地輓歌》和阿諾德的《多佛海濱》均為千古絕唱,可謂抒寫了"有我之境",但創造的意境大相徑庭:葛雷以薄暮時蕭瑟蒼涼的墓園氣氛烘托哀思,阿諾德有感於月夜海邊時起時伏的濤聲,而曲傳悒鬱幽怨的思緒。相形之下,美國詩人較為開朗,譬如朗費羅的《金色夕照》也描繪黃昏景色,却明快燦爛,同葛雷的詩形成鮮明的對照。

至於詩的風格,從傳統來講也不外乎兩

---

[1] 見王國維著《人間詞話》卷上,頁1;中華書局,1957年。

[2] 見嚴羽著《滄浪詩話·詩辨篇》及王士禛著《池北偶談》、《帶經堂詩話·答問類》。

類,即我國歷代詩話所謂豪放與婉約,西方古典文藝理論槪括的崇高(the Sublime)和秀美(the Beautiful)。誠然,眞正的詩人各有獨創的風格,如約翰・鄧恩的詩句剛健而峭刻(hard lines),"骨勁而氣猛"(引《文心雕龍・風骨篇》);本集選譯的《死神莫驕妄》一詩顯然反映了這種"風骨"。對比之下,彌爾頓的詩風華嚴雄渾,斯賓塞絢麗,馬羅恢宏;靈秀如雪萊,蘊藉如濟慈,沉鬱如霍思曼;丹尼生韵律謹嚴,鑄詞煉句精工而華贍;白朗寧繪聲繪影,戲劇性特强;斯溫本音節諧婉,埃默生雅人深致,羅賽蒂兄妹要眇宜修。莎士比亞則兼備衆美,即使從這裏選的六首十四行詩,也能領略其豐富多彩的風格。總之,從這一簡編中,各家的詩風可見一斑。

在詩歌創作同理論的關係上,可以說詩人寫作時或多或少、有意無意地(無意者居多)實踐或符合某種文藝觀點。譬如西方早期較爲系統化的詩論,亞里斯多德的講稿《詩學》要點之一是"摹仿論",第六章有具體的闡述:"摹仿的方式是借人物的動作來表達……借引起憐憫與恐懼來使這種情感得到陶冶。"[1]("陶冶"是Katharsis的譯文,或譯"淨化",

---

[1] 引自亞里斯多德著《詩學》,羅念生譯,頁19;人民文學出版社,1982年。(這一譯本內尚有楊周翰譯的賀拉斯作《詩藝》。)

"宣泄"。)這是指悲劇而言(《詩學》基本上不談抒情詩),但也適用於各種體裁的詩歌。例如本集所選朱湘譯的柯爾律奇長篇幻想叙事詩《老舟子行》(*The Rime of the Ancient Mariner,* 1798),以及現實主義詩人托馬斯·霍特的名篇《襯衫之歌》,在不同程度內都符合上述論點。但在題材與技巧上,兩首詩截然不同。前者以汪洋恣肆的想象力,淋漓盡致地描摹了老水手在海上離奇而險惡的經歷,驚心動魄,確能引起憐憫和恐懼之感;後者則懷着由衷的同情,以白描手法咏述縫衣女在貧富懸殊的資本主義社會裏淒慘的遭遇,字字血淚,激起讀者憐憫而又悲憤的心情。

　　柯爾律奇的那首長詩也實踐了他本人的論點:以逼真而富於人情味的方式,描寫詭奇的幻景、異國情調和浪漫的奇人奇事,從而令人"情願暫時信以為真"(willing suspension of disbelief)。[1]這一觀點有別於崇尚自然的沃茲沃斯提出的論點:詩歌起源於"在寧靜中回憶的情感"(emotion recollected in tranquility)。[2]本集內沃氏的名作《水仙》與

---

[1] 見柯爾律奇著《文學評傳》(*Literaria Biographia*)第14章。
[2] 見沃茲沃斯作《抒情謠曲1800年再版序》,載E.D. Jones編 *English Critical Essays: Nineteenth Century*,頁26。

《威斯敏斯特橋上有感》充分體現了他的理論。

然而,上述柯爾律奇的浪漫主義觀點同另一位浪漫主義詩人濟慈的名言"消極功能"(negative capability,或譯"天然接受力")却有相通的含意。濟慈於1817年12月21日在致兄弟喬治和托馬斯的信裏寫道:"使一個人,尤其是文人,卓有成就的品質乃是消極功能;莎士比亞富有這種品質,達到極大的程度;那就是說,一個人能處於迷惘、神秘和惶惑之中,而毫不煩心地去考慮事實與理性……在一位大詩人心目裏,美感超過以至消除其他任何想法。"(1)這不僅是浪漫的而且是唯美的論調,同本集所選濟慈的詩《希臘古甕頌》內咏述的"美即眞,眞即美"的道理是一致的。詩中讚美的對象——希臘古甕上描繪的情景:綠蔭下,俊美的小伙子熱烈追求含羞而躲避的少女,通過濟慈的名篇而流傳後世,並且這首詩或許比那畫像更生動、更饒有韵味。正如萊辛闡明的:"畫家只能暗示動態……但是在詩裏,媚却保持它的本色,它是一種稍縱即逝而令人百看不厭的美。"(2)確實,濟慈雋永的詩

---

(1) 引自《濟慈書信選》(*Selected Letters of John Keats*),李昂奈爾·屈列林(Lionel Trilling)編,頁103;紐約,德卜爾台(Doubleday)出版公司,1956年。

(2) 引自萊辛著《拉奧孔》,朱光潛譯,頁121;人民文學出版社,1982年。

歌是百咏不厭的。他的審美感極其敏銳,格調高,藝術性濃郁。吟誦其詩彷彿飲醇酒,回味無窮。因此,當前西方文學界對濟慈的評價愈來愈高了。

可是,這位詩人的見解未免偏激(這也是浪漫主義者的本色吧)。譬如他說莎士比亞富於極大的"消極功能",只說對了一半。固然,莎士比亞能深切地感受迷惘和惆悵的情緒,並表達得非常動人,如本集選的六首十四行詩。但是,在遭到"衆人唾棄"、自怨自艾之後,或在回憶悲痛的往事之後,詩人便筆鋒一轉,借理想的對象而表示樂觀的希望和欣悅的信心了。事實上,伊麗莎白時期這位最傑出的詩人和戲劇家,無論在創作或實際生活裏,都保持了理智同感情的高度平衡,否則他不可能在戲劇創作和社會活動兩方面都獲得巨大的成功。

莎士比亞喜劇《仲夏夜之夢》第五幕第一場內,有一段台詞極爲精闢地描述了詩人創作的特徵:在狂熱的幻想中,目光四射,上天入地,觀察大千世界(Doth glance from heaven to earth, from earth to heaven);爾後把想象中空靈的事物具體而眞切地描繪,變成形象(…the poet's pen/Turns them to shapes…),並賦予地點和名稱(…gives to airy nothing/A local habitation and a name.)。這段話雖然簡括,却講得異常透徹,把詩歌創作中豐盈的想象力、強烈的感情、銳利的觀察,以及精細和真實的刻劃,均有機地聯結起來,也就是感情與理智的融合。同濟慈的說法相比,顯得更深刻而全面了。

其實,濟慈拈出的"消極功能"倒更適合約翰·鄧恩的性格及其作品,比如本集選譯的《塵世剖析》幾節,把"開天闢地"以來的人世間,描寫爲"一團混沌","了無理性、邏輯"等等,表現了極端的迷惘和陰郁的絕望,以及憤世嫉俗的心情。可以說,在這位玄學派(the metaphysical poets)鼻祖的思想感情裏,在某些方面,"消極功能"達到了飽和點,莫怪許多厭世的現代派詩人與文人要奉他爲"大宗師"了。

同上述消極的觀點相反,文學理論中歷來有很多積極的論點。譬如西方早期文論中,古羅馬修辭學家和文藝批評家朗加納斯(或譯郎吉弩斯,Cassius Longinus, 213—273)在其著作《論崇高》內闡述的要點是有積極意義的。作者在第五章裏列舉了崇高語言的五個來源,並強調說:"第一而且最重要的是莊嚴偉大的思想……第二是強烈而激動的情感。"他在這一章結尾時總結道:"崇高的第五個因素總結全部上述四個,就是整個結構的堂皇卓越。"[1]

---

[1] 引自《西方文論選》上卷,伍蠡甫主編,頁125;
上海文藝出版社,1963年。

這些見解極其精當。如以詩人的作品為例,彌爾頓的史詩就符合上述幾點。這位情操高潔、思想激進的大詩人在不朽之作《失樂園》裏,塑造了撒但悲壯的形象,表達了堅決反抗專制的英雄精神,從而體現了"莊嚴偉大的思想"。同時,史詩的總體結構(the architectonic)堪稱"堂皇卓越"。在本集所選彌爾頓的四首短篇抒情詩、哲理詩和悼亡詩內,儘管這些特點不太顯著,但字裏行間也令人感到崇高的素質。至於"強烈而激動的情感",在彌爾頓的詩篇裏較為含蓄,而在浪漫主義詩人彭斯、雪萊與拜倫等的作品中明顯得多了。

就雪萊而言,他不僅在詩歌裏抒發熾烈的情感,並且以詩人的慧眼預見未來,描繪理想的前景。《西風頌》便是典型的例證,結尾以嚴冬和陽春為隱喻的名句,幾乎傳遍人間了。事實上,詩人實踐了自己的理論,因為他在《詩辯》一文中明確地主張:詩人既是"立法者"(legislator),又是"先知"(prophet),故不僅能"看透當前的眞相"(…beholds intensely the present as it is…),並且能"在當今預見未來。"(…beholds the future in the present…)[1]

---

[1] 引自雪萊作《詩辯》,見 E. D. Jones 編 *English Critical Essays: Nineteenth Century*, 頁124。

這種預見性在另一位浪漫主義奇才布萊克的詩中也顯示出來。他是雪萊等激進民主主義者的先驅，比雪萊（至少比拜倫）更淳樸。因爲他是銅版雕匠，本人是平民，深知被壓迫人民的苦難，故而不僅懷着眞摯的同情（參閱選詩《掃烟囱的小孩》），而且在詩歌內發出憤慨的呼聲，預言革命風暴。本集所選布萊克的名篇《老虎》是有代表性的作品，不但具有象徵意味，並含有預言的性質。詩人以斬截突兀、鏗鏘有力的節奏（稱爲anvil music——"砧樂"，即錘鐵般的音調）塑造了"猛虎"雄偉而可怖的形象，可能象徵革命的暴力，預示着震撼天地的力量。儘管這首詩同布萊克的其他詩篇一樣，帶有神秘的宗敎色彩（常用《聖經》的故事、人物以至詞語），實際上却富於強烈的民主主義精神。這和布萊克深受法國大革命的影響並始終堅決擁護是有密切關係的。

　　布萊克的後期作品更富有預示性。事實上，他把後期的詩結集而題名爲《先知書》（*Prophetic Books*），其中包括《法國革命》（1791）與《歐洲：一篇預言》（*Europe: A Prophesy,* 1794）等。這些詩歌借《聖經》的傳說宣傳泛神論，預言未來革新的美好的社會。

　　在詩歌發展的長河中，另有比上述各種作品更切實和嚴肅的，即富於現實意義或寓有道德意味的詩篇。這類詩較爲直接地刻劃現實生活,揭露社會矛盾,諷刺與抨擊黑暗和罪惡,或憂時愛國,反映民生疾苦,或壯懷激烈,充滿反抗暴虐與侵略的戰鬥精神。這類詩源遠流長,深入人心,滙成洪流,在文藝領域內起着推動歷史的作用。在我國,這種詩可追溯至《詩經》(如《七月》,《邶風·北門》等)與《楚辭》(屈原賦《離騷》、《哀郢》、《懷沙》等)。以後如蔡琰的悲憤詩(關於此詩作者尚有爭議),魏武慷慨蒼涼的詩篇,建安七子哀嘆亂離的仿樂府詩;尤其是阮籍和嵇康、劉琨與左思等風骨彌高、雄峻而沉痛的"叙喪亂"之詩。爾後可舉犖犖大者,如杜甫詩(三吏、三別等),白居易的諷喻詩,陸游的愛國詩,辛棄疾與陳亮詞等。近代如龔自珍、譚嗣同和黃遵憲(《人境廬詩草》)等抨擊腐朽沒落的頑固勢力以及列強侵入而奮發圖強的詩歌。

總之,這類詩大都符合白居易倡言的鮮明論點:"文章合爲時而著,歌詩合爲事而作。"(《新樂府·序》)並且在不同程度上,融合了"詩言志"同"文以載道"的傳統觀點;因爲封建時代詩人與文人基本上都深受儒家思想的薰陶和覊勒,不可能徹底逾越藩籬,雖然有不少詩人兼有佛、道的傾向。相對而言,儒家入世的學說總是佔主導地位,即使鍾嶸稱爲"隱逸詩人之宗"的陶潛也曾詠懷云:"先師有遺訓,憂道不憂貧。"(《癸卯歲始春懷古田舍》)

在西方,從荷馬史詩以及希臘悲劇與喜劇(廣義地說都是詩劇)開始,便有關於當時社會生活多方面的描述,儘管那些古代傑作大都以神話與傳說為素材。經過漫長的黑暗的中世紀,到了借復古之名、行革新之實的輝煌的文藝復興時代,從先驅者喬叟發軔,在《坎特伯雷故事集》裏以詩的形式描摹世態,譏諷教會、僧侶和禁慾主義,栩栩如生地刻劃英國資本主義萌芽期的眾生相。之後,馬羅、莎士比亞與本·瓊生等在詩劇中,進一步深入而廣泛地描寫錯綜複雜、劇烈動蕩的社會面貌,雖然常以古羅馬、意大利與丹麥等為背景。他們用詩的彩筆描繪了人文主義為主流的時代精神的巨幅畫卷。

以後,歌德的劃時代史詩《浮士德》以巨匠的手腕融合了理想同現實、"詩與真"[1]。海涅、雨果、貝朗瑞和鮑狄埃等歐洲大陸詩人,彭斯、戈爾司密斯(參閱其名作《荒村》)、拜倫與雪萊等英國詩人,以及美國詩人惠特曼、桑德堡、弗洛斯特和黑人詩人休斯等,大都在作品中交織着浪漫主義的或革命的理想與熱情,以及反映社會矛盾跟鬥爭的真實描寫。普希金和萊蒙托夫所作的針砭暴政、渴望自由的詩歌,馬雅柯夫斯基洋溢着戰鬥精神的梯形詩,

---

[1] 借用歌德自傳題名 *Dichtung und Wahrheit*。

勃洛克謳歌十月革命的象徵詩（《十二個》）等等，也具有上述特徵。

總而言之，優秀的詩人同戲劇家、小說家一樣，往往在作品裏有機地結合現實主義和浪漫主義，以至古典主義與象徵主義的因素，難以機械地區別。誠然，各個作家的主要傾向與創作方法不同，或在生平某一時期以現實主義為主，另一時期則偏重浪漫主義。譬如海涅前期大多寫悱惻動人、柔情如水的抒情詩，如1827年出版的《歌集》中抒唱大自然和愛情的詩篇，充盈着浪漫情調；後期的創作，如1843年發表的《德國——一個冬天的童話》，却富於犀利的諷刺、機趣橫生的比喻，以及鮮明的現實性。

又如拜倫主要是浪漫派詩人，但後期的長篇叙事詩《唐·璜》（尤其後半部）則充滿辛辣的諷刺，以現實主義手法尖銳地揭露紳士淑女的市儈習氣（philistinism）、偽善的面貌和醜惡的本性。本集所選《恰爾德·哈洛德漫遊記》第三卷著名片段《滑鐵盧前夜》，也運用現實主義筆法再現歷史場景，繪聲繪影，極逼真之能事。

再如現代派重要詩人艾略特（T. S. Eliot, 1888－1965），自然在創作中有現代主義的特點，例如用含蓄或隱晦的象徵性意象（symbolic imagery）描述現代西方資本主義社會普遍的異化（alienation），以片斷的叙述（fragmented narration)與內心獨白(interior monologue)、時空交錯或顛倒(time travelling)等技巧，深入挖掘現代人彷徨和絕望的心理狀態。然而，艾略特實質上是個古典主義者，對古典文化有深湛的修養，因而在其代表作《荒原》（*The Waste Land*, 1922）與《四闋四重奏》（*Four Quartets*, 1944）內，能駕輕就熟地大量引用典故。並且，這些長詩似乎支離破碎，其實結構謹嚴，乃是古典派的特色。此外，艾略特的文體明晰而凝煉，也是古典風格。所有這些特徵充分體現在他的詩劇《大敎堂謀殺案》，特別在其論著《傳統與個人才智》、《論詩劇》和《論玄學派》等文章裏。事實上，他本人曾宣稱："在政治上我是保皇派，在宗教上我是天主教徒，在文藝創作上我是古典主義者。"或許可以說，艾略特的現代派詩歌是一種古典變奏曲吧。

在選譯的近代詩中，霍特的《襯衫之歌》同憲章派詩人瓊斯等的作品具有迫切的現實意義；由於時代更近，唸起來比上述較古的詩更爲親切。憲章派詩歌特別可貴，因爲在西方詩壇上，這些作品首先直截了當喊出了被剝削的勞工的呼聲。雖然在技巧上不像專業詩人那麼講究，但態度鮮明得多，感情更眞、更樸實，因此在一定意義上，更能打動人心。

本集所選每個詩人作品之後,均附簡介。主要為了使讀者了解各個詩人的生平,創作概況與特色。大部份詩加必要的註解,主要是譯者所註,有些是編者補註。如有不當之處,請讀者示知,俾能改善。

凡已正式發表的譯詩(載於詩集或刊物),一律照錄,只校不改;未曾發表者,如有筆誤或不妥之處,試予酌改,不盡中肯,敬祈譯者鑒諒。

按原來計劃,入選的詩中有若干長篇,如郭沫若譯雪萊詩《雲鳥曲》等;後因限於篇幅,有些只得割愛,如楚圖南譯惠特曼詩《斧頭之歌》;另一些則節選,如朱湘譯柯爾律奇詩《老舟子行》,等等。嘗鼎一臠,未免割裂之虞,尚希原宥。

限於客觀條件,未能事先一一徵求譯者同意轉載,請予諒解,並致歉意。

這本詩選主要供詩歌愛好者鑒賞,也可作為高等院校英美文學課程的參考讀物或教材。

在擬訂計劃與編選過程中,承尊敬的方重老學長關懷與指點;在搜集資料方面,蒙吳鈞陶先生熱情地賜助;願二位不嫌微末地接受編者衷心的謝忱。本書有關材料的整理、打字與複印,承上海外語教育出版社編輯部同仁大力幫助,特致以衷心的感謝。

詩國無邊而編者譾陋,掛一漏萬在所難

免;入選者未必允當,或輕重倒置,比例失調;詮釋涉及頗廣,"但恨謬誤多",統希讀者與海內外方家匡正。

> 孫梁
> 1985年仲夏
> 於禺廬,上海

CONTENTS

《一百叢書》總序 ································· 1
前言 ··· 1

Geoffrey Chaucer 杰弗雷·喬叟
 1 Cantus Troili 特羅勒斯的情歌 ················· 2
 2 Lenvoy de Chaucer 喬叟的詩跋 ················ 6
 3 Fortune 幸運箴 ··························· 10
 4 Moral Balade of Gentilesse 高貴的品質 ········ 18
 5 The Complaint of Chaucer to His Purse 喬叟的怨詩致錢囊 ······························· 22

Thomas Wyatt 托馬斯·韋艾特
 6 Forget Not Yet 別忘了 ····················· 26

Walter Raleigh 華爾特·拉雷
 7 The Silent Lover 沉默的戀人 ················ 30

Edmund Spenser 埃德蒙·斯賓塞
 8 Whilst It Is Prime 行樂當及時 ·············· 32
 9 Sweet Is the Rose 玫瑰多美呵 ··············· 34

Philip Sidney 菲力普·錫特尼
 10 A Ditty 謠曲 ····························· 36

Christopher Marlowe 克利斯朵夫·馬羅
 11 Nature 大自然 ···························· 38
 12 The Passionate Shepherd to His Love 熱烈的牧人情歌 ································· 40

William Shakespeare 威廉·莎士比亞
     Selected Sonnets 十四行詩選

1

13 Shall I Compare Thee to a Summer's Day(XVIII) 能否把你比作夏日璀璨(第十八首)······················44

14 When in Disgrace with Fortune and Men's Eyes (XXIX) 可嘆時運不濟衆人唾棄(第二十九首)········46

15 When to the Sessions of Sweet Silent Thought (XXX) 在寧謐的沉思中憶往昔(第三十首)············48

16 Not Marble, Not the Gilded Monuments (LV) 沒有雲石或王公們金的墓碑(第五十五首)················50

17 Since Brass, nor Stone, nor Earth, nor Boundless Sea (LXV) 旣然是鐵石，大地，無邊的海洋(第六十五首)··52

18 When in the Chronicle of Wasted Time (CVI) 過往世代的記載裏常常見到(第一〇六首)················54

Thomas Nashe 托馬斯・納希
19 Spring 春 ··56

John Donne 約翰・鄧恩
20 Death Be Not Proud 死神莫驕妄 ·····················58
21 An Anatomie of the World (Extract) 塵世剖析(節選)··60

Ben Jonson 本・瓊生
22 To the Memory of My Beloved, the Author Mr. William Shakespeare And What He Hath Left Us 題威廉・莎士比亞先生的遺著，紀念吾敬愛的作者 ··66

Robert Herrick 羅伯特・海立克
23 To the Virgins, to Make Much of Time 勸女于歸 ··74

John Milton 約翰・彌爾頓
24 On His Deceased Wife 夢亡妻······················76

25　To Cyriack Skinner 給西里亞克・斯基納 ………… *78*
26　On His Blindness 關於他的瞎眼 ………………… *80*
27　Light 向光呼籲 ……………………………………… *82*

John Dryden 約翰・屈拉頓
28　Epigram on Milton 題彌爾頓畫像 ……………… *86*

Alexander Pope 亞歷山大・蒲伯
29　Ode on Solitude 隱居頌 ………………………… *88*

Thomas Gray 托馬斯・葛雷
30　Elegy Written in a Country Churchyard (Extract)
　　鄉村墓地輓歌（節選）………………………………… *92*

William Cowper 威廉・柯珀
31　My Mary 我的瑪麗 ………………………………… *96*

William Blake 威廉・布萊克
32　Reeds of Innocence 天眞之歌 ………………… *102*
33　The Tiger 老虎 …………………………………… *106*
34　The Chimney Sweeper 掃烟囪的小孩 ……… *110*

Robert Burns 羅伯特・彭斯
35　My Heart's in the Highlands 我的心呀在高原 … *112*
36　'A Man's a Man for A' That 不管那一套 ……… *116*
37　Scots Wha Ha'e 蘇格蘭人 ……………………… *120*
38　A Red, Red Rose 一朵紅紅的玫瑰 …………… *124*
39　John Anderson, My Jo 約翰・安徒生，我愛 … *126*

William Wordsworth 威廉・沃玆沃斯
40　Lucy Gray 露西抒情詩 …………………………… *128*
41　The Solitary Reaper 孤獨的割禾女 …………… *130*
42　The Daffodils 水仙 ……………………………… *134*
43　Upon Westminster Bridge 威斯敏斯特橋上有感.. *138*
44　To the Cuckoo 致布穀鳥 ……………………… *140*

Walter Scott 華爾德・司各特

45　Hunting Song 行獵歌 ……………………… *144*
　　46　The Pride of Youth 青春的驕傲……………… *148*
Samuel Taylor Coleridge 賽繆爾・泰勒・柯爾律奇
　　47　The Rime of the Ancient Mariner (Extract) 老舟子行(節選)……………………………………… *150*
Walter Savage Landor 沃爾特・薩凡基・蘭德
　　48　Finis 終曲 ……………………………………… *168*
George Gordon Byron 喬治・戈登・拜倫
　　49　There Was a Sound of Revelry by Night 滑鐵盧前夜……………………………………………… *170*
　　50　When We Two Parted 昔日依依別…………… *174*
　　51　Childe Harold's Pilgrimage Canto I:XIII (Interlude) 《恰爾德・哈洛德漫遊記》第一卷第十三節(插曲)‥ *178*
　　52　The Isles of Greece 希臘羣島……………… *186*
Percy Bysshe Shelley 波西・比希・雪萊
　　53　Ode to the West Wind 西風頌……………… *198*
　　54　Ozymandias 奧西曼提斯…………………… *208*
　　55　To— 致— ……………………………………… *210*
　　56　Rise Like Lions 像醒獅般奮起………………… *212*
　　57　Music, When Soft Voices Die 輕柔的聲音寂滅後
　　　　………………………………………………… *214*
John Keats 約翰・濟慈
　　58　Ode to a Nightingale 夜鶯頌………………… *216*
　　59　Ode on a Grecian Urn 希臘古甕頌…………… *224*
　　60　La Belle Dame sans Merci 無情的妖女……… *230*
　　61　The Grasshopper and the Cricket 蟈蟈與蟋蟀… *236*
Thomas Hood 托馬斯・霍特
　　62　The Song of the Shirt 襯衫之歌……………… *238*
Ralph Waldo Emerson 拉爾夫・華爾多・埃默生

63 The Apology 辯白 ········· *248*

Elizabeth Barret Browning 伊麗莎白·巴萊特·白朗寧

64 Sonnets from the Portuguese：I 抒情十四行詩選：一 ········ *252*

65 Sonnets from the Portuguese：III 抒情十四行詩選：三 ········ *254*

Henry Wadsworth Longfellow 亨利·瓦茨沃斯·朗費羅

66 A Psalm of Life 生之讚歌 ········ *256*

67 My Lost Youth 我失去的青春 ········ *260*

68 The Arrow and the Song 箭和歌 ········ *270*

69 The Golden Sunset 金色夕照 ········ *272*

Edgar Allan Poe 埃特加·阿倫·坡

70 Annabel Lee 安娜貝·李 ········ *276*

Edward Fitzgerald 愛德華·菲茲吉拉德

71 The Rubáiyát of Omar Khayyám of Naishápúr (Extract) 莪默·伽亞謨作《魯拜集》(節選) ········ *282*

Alfred Tennyson 阿爾弗雷德·丹尼生

72 Break, Break, Break 拍岸曲 ········ *288*

73 Crossing the Bar 渡沙渚 ········ *290*

74 Sweet and Low 輕輕地，柔和地 ········ *292*

Robert Browning 羅伯特·白朗寧

75 Home-Thoughts, from the Sea 海上鄉思 ········ *294*

76 Home-Thoughts, from Abroad 海外鄉思 ········ *296*

77 Pippa's Song 比芭之歌 ········ *298*

James Russell Lowell 詹姆斯·羅塞爾·洛威爾

78 The Fountain 噴泉 ········ *300*

Walt Whitman 瓦爾特·惠特曼

79 I Hear America Singing 我聽見美利堅在歌唱 ···· *304*

80 I Saw in Louisiana a Live-Oak Growing 在路易

斯安那我看見一棵槲樹 ················· *306*
81　O Captain! My Captain! 啊，船長！我的船長！.. *308*
82　Two Rivulets 雙溪 ························· *312*
83　The Dalliance of the Eagles 鷹的調情 ········· *314*

Ernest Jones 歐內斯特・瓊斯
84　The Song of the Wage-Slaves 工資奴隸之歌 ····· *316*

Matthew Arnold 麥修・阿諾德
85　Dover Beach 多佛海濱 ······················ *322*
86　Memorial Verses (Extract) 悼詩（節選）········· *326*

Dante Gabriel Rossetti 但丁・加百列爾・羅賽蒂
87　Three Shadows 三重影 ······················· *330*

Christina Georgina Rossetti 克里斯蒂娜・喬金娜・羅賽蒂
88　A Pause 逗留 ································ *332*
89　When I Am Dead, My Dearest 當我離開人間，最親愛的 ································ *334*

Emily Dickinson 艾米利・狄更遜
90　Little Stone 小石 ····························· *336*
91　Presentiment 預感 ··························· *338*
92　I'm Nobody 我是無名之輩 ··················· *340*

Algernon Charles Swinburne 阿爾杰農・查爾斯・斯溫本
93　A Match 配偶 ······························· *342*
94　Love at Sea 海上的愛情 ····················· *348*

Alfred Edward Houseman 阿爾弗萊德・愛德華・霍思曼
95　Reveille 起身號 ····························· *352*
96　Bring, in This Timeless Grave to Throw 雪中莫去折黯淡的柏枝 ····················· *356*
97　When I Came Last to Ludlow 上次我回到祿如鎮
　　································ *360*
98　Hughley Steeple 休來寺 ······················ *362*

Edward Thomas 愛德華・托馬斯
  99 The Pond 池 ………………………………… *366*
  100 July 七月 ……………………………………… *368*
Bibliography 參考書目 ………………………………… *370*

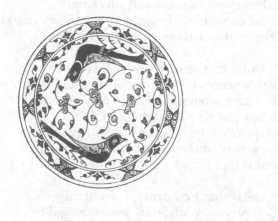

1 Cantus Troili

Geoffrey Chaucer

"If no love is, O God, what fele I so?
And if love is, what thing and whiche is he?
If love be good, from whennes comth my wo?
If it be wikke, a wonder thinketh me,
When every torment and adversitee
That cometh of him, may to me savory thinke;
For ay thurst I, the more that I it drinke.

"And if that at myn owene lust I brenne,
Fro whennes cometh my wailing and my pleynte?
If harme agree me, wher-to pleyne I thenne?
I noot, ne why unwery that I faynte.
O quike deeth, o swete harm so queynte,
How may of thee in me swich quantitee,
But if that I consente that it be?

"And if that I consente, I wrongfully
Compleyne, y-wis; thus possed to and fro,
Al sterelees withinne a boot am I
Amid the see, bytwixen windes two,

喬叟(1340?－1400)，生於倫敦，父親為酒商。1372至1381年間多次奉命赴意大利、法國等地進行外交事務。喬叟以中古英語創作詩歌，為英國詩體奠定基礎，稱為"英國詩歌之父"。

一 特羅勒斯的情歌

杰弗雷·喬叟

假使愛不存在,天哪,我所感受的是什麽?
　　假使愛存在,它究竟是怎樣一件東西?
假使愛是好的,我的悲哀何從而降落?
假使愛是壞的,我想却有些希奇,
　　哪管它帶來了多少苦難和乖戾,
好似生命之源,竟能引起我無限快感;
　　使我愈喝得多,愈覺得口裏燥乾。

如果我已在歡樂中活躍,
　　又何處來這愁訴和悲號?
如果災害能與我相容,何不破涕爲笑?
　　我要請問,旣未疲勞,何以會暈倒?
　　　啊,生中之死,啊,禍害迷人眞奇巧,
若不是我自己給了你許可,
　　你怎敢重重疊疊壓在我心頭。

可是我若許可了,我就不該
　　再作苦訴。我終日漂蕩,
像在無舵的船中浮海,
　　無邊無岸,吹着相反的風向,

《特羅勒斯的情歌》選自長詩 *Troilus and Criseyde*, 共分三節,每節韻脚按 ababbcc 排列,稱爲"皇家曲調"。

That in contrarie stonden evermo.
Allas! what is this wonder maladye?
For hete of cold, for cold of hete, I dye."

永遠如此漂逐，忽下又忽上。
呀，這是一種什麼奇特的病徵，
　冷中發熱，熱中發冷，斷送我生命。

方重譯

2 Lenvoy de Chaucer

Geoffrey Chaucer

Grisilde is deed, and eek hir pacience,
And bothe atones buried in Itaille;
For which I crye in open audience,
No wedded man so hardy be t'assaille
His wyves pacience, in hope to finde
Grisildes, for in certein he shall faille!

O noble wyves, ful of heigh prudence,
Lat noon humilitee your tonge naille,
Ne lat no clerk have cause or diligence
To wryte of yow a storie of swich mervaille
As of Grisildis pacient and kinde;
Lest Chichevache yow swelwe in hir entraille!

Folweth Ekko, that holdeth no silence,
But evere answereth at the countretaille;
Beth nat bidaffed for your innocence,
But sharply tak on yow the governaille.
Emprinteth wel this lesson in your minde

　　《喬叟的詩跋》選自長詩 *The Canterbury Tales*,
共六段，每段六行。二、四、六行押韻，十八行一韻
到底；一、三行押韻，十二行一韻到底；各段第五行

二 喬叟的詩跋

杰弗雷・喬叟

格麗西達死了,連同她的一片真誠,
　　都已葬進了意大利的土壤;
因此我要向衆人高呼一聲,
　　願天下做丈夫的人不論怎樣頑强,
　　　不可試探他的妻,或想找到
　　第二個格麗西達,那是不可能了。

啊,高貴的妻子們,聰明的妻子們,
　　勿讓謙卑釘緊了你們的舌尖,
勿使學者們有所藉口,
　　再來寫這樣一篇奇事,
　　　像溫順的格麗西達一樣,
　　當心瘦牛(1)把你們吞下肚子。

學習回音女神,她是永不停舌的,
　　她在山間谷底永遠回話傳語;
莫太天眞,或由人欺侮,
　　堅決掌握着治家之權。
　　　深深記取這個對人們的敎訓,

―――――――

另屬一韻。
(1) 古代法國寓言中一隻巨大瘦牛,專吞卑順的妻子,
　　愈吞愈瘦。

For commune profit, sith it may availle.

Ye archewyves, atondeth at defence,
Synye be strong as is a greet camaille;
Ne suffreth nat that men yow doon offence.
And sclendre wyves, feble as in bataille,
Beth egre as is a tygre yond in Inde;
Ay clappeth as a mille, I yow consaille.

Ne dreed hem nat, do hem no reverence;
For though thyn housbonde armed be in maille,
The arwes of thy crabbed eloquence
Shal perce his brest, and eek his aventaille;
In jalousye I rede eek thou him binde,
And thou shalt make hym couche as dooth a quaille.

If thou be fair, ther folk ben in presence
Shew thou thy visage and thyn apparaille;
If thou be foul, be free of thy dispence,
To gete thee freendes ay do thy travaille;
Be ay of chere as light as leef on linde,
And lat him care, and wepe and wringe, and waille!

為了人人的利益，自可不必疑慮。

你們悍婦們，永遠捍衛着自身，
　你們像一隻駱駝那樣健壯；
莫讓男子們欺凌你們。
　你們瘦小的妻媳們，經不起一擊，
　　學習那印度的猛虎，
　我勸你們，像風車一樣作響。

不要害怕男子，不要禮敬，
　雖然你的丈夫滿身甲冑，
你那詆譭的舌箭，會刺進
　他的胸膛，擊中他的面盔，
　　再用嫉妒把你丈夫繫住，
　可使他們偃伏，像一隻鵪鶉。

如果你長得美，你不妨到處遊逛，
　你可以擺出你的容貌和衣飾；
如果你長得醜，花錢應慷慨
　盡量結交朋友，不要緊縮。
　　放鬆你的心情，像樹顛一葉；
　由他們男子去激怒、絞腸和哭泣。

　　　　　　　　　　　　方重譯

3 Fortune

Balades de visage sanz peinture

Geoffrey Chaucer

I Le Pleintif countre Fortune

This wrecched worldes transmutacioun,
As wele or wo, now povre and now honour,
Withouten ordre or wys discrecioun
Governed is by Fortunes errour.
But natheles, the lak of hir favour
Ne may nat don me singen, though I dye,
"Jay tout perdu mon temps et mon labour;"
For fynally, Fortune, I thee defye!

Yit is me left the light of my resoun,
To knowen frend fro fo in thy mirour.
So muchel hath yit thy whirling up and doun
Ytaught me for to knowen in an hour.
But trewely, no force of thy reddour
To him that over himself hath the mays trye!
My suffisaunce shal be my socour;
For fynally, Fortune, I thee defye!

三　幸運辯

歌頌一個忠實的朋友(1)

杰弗雷・喬叟

一　控告幸運

這條險惡的世途何其多故，
　　眞是朝秦暮楚，禍福不停留，
一切聽憑幸運去任意擺佈，
　　並沒有任何章法，或半點理由。
可是哪怕你對我用心如何，
　　我總不會死心塌地向你哭啼，
唱什麼"我的時光和精力全付東流"；
　　老實對你講，幸運，你不在我眼裏！

我心中留下了一點理性之光，
　　使我在你那千變萬化的鏡頭上，
仍能辨別敵友。雖然世事滄桑，
　　正好叫我學得聰明，不上你的當。
人能掌握自己，就不會對你賣賬！
　　你的殘酷行爲不能使我驚奇，
因我既胸有成竹就有了保障；
　　老實對你講，幸運，你不在我眼裏！

本篇應爲1380年以後的作品。
(1)這位"忠實的朋友"及詩中的"摯友"指詩人的護主或理查王。

O Socrates, thou stidfast champioun,
She never mighte be thy tormentour;
Thou never dreddest hir oppressioun,
Ne in hir chere founde thou no savour.
Thou knewe wel the deceit of hir colour,
And that hir moste worshipe is to lye.
I knowe hir eek a fals dissimulour;
For fynally, Fortune, I thee defye!

II   La respounse de Fortune au Pleintif

No man is wrecched, but himself it wene,
And he that hath himself hath suffisaunce.
Why seystow thanne I am to thee so kene,
That hast thyself out of my governaunce?
Sey thus: "Graunt mercy of thyn haboundaunce
That thou hast lent or this." Why wolt thou stryve?
What wostow yit how I thee wol avaunce?
And eek thou hast thy beste frend alyve.

I have thee taught divisioun bitwene
Frend of effect, and frend of countenaunce;
Thee nedeth nat the galle of noon hyene,
That cureth eyen derked for penaunce;
Now seestow cleer, that were in ignoraunce.
Yit halt thyn ancre, and yit thou mayst arryve

啊，蘇格拉底，你是百折不撓的戰士，
　　幸運無法在你身上施展淫威；
你不害怕她對你任何壓制，
　　她的花言巧語也不會叫你吃虧。
你看破了她一切的色澤光輝，
　　她以欺詐作榮，你却能置之不理。
我也懂得她總是謊話一大批；
　　老實對你講，幸運，你不在我眼裏！

二　幸運答辯

誰都不會倒霉，除非你自認無能，
　　凡人能自有把握，方得事事如意。
如果你相信已遠離了我的禁城，
　　為什麼又說我待你過於嚴厲？
你向我求道，"願你寬恩護庇，
　　像你過去一般。"那你又何須鬥爭？
為你的前途你怎知我將如何提携？
　　何況，你還有摯友在為你關心。

我曾教過你認清眞實的朋友，
　　一個假獻殷勤的人最不可靠；
人若眼睛失明往往要利用鬣狗
　　將它的苦胆治病，你倒無此需要；
因你雖一度模糊，現已能觀察精到。
　　你駕駛何等平穩，必然安渡迷津，

Ther bountee berth the keye of my substaunce;
And eek thou hast thy beste frend alyve.

How many have I refused to sustene,
Sin I thee fostred have in thy plesaunce!
Woltow than make a statut on thy quene
That I shal been ay at thyn ordinaunce?
Thou born art in my regne of variaunce,
Aboute the wheel with other most thou dryve.
My lore is bet than wikke is thy grevaunce
And eek thou hast thy beste frend alyve.

III *La respounse du Pleintif countre Fortune*

Thy lore I dampne, it is adversitee.
My frend maystow nat reven, blind goddesse!
That I thy frendes knowe, I thanke hit thee.
Tak hem agayn, lat hem go lye on presse!
The negardye in keping hir richesse
Prenostik is thou wolt hir tour assayle;
Wikke appetyt comth ay before syknesse:
In general, this reule may nat fayle.

La respounse de Fortune countre le Pleintif

Thou pinchest at my mutabilitee,
For I thee lente a drope of my richesse,
And now me lyketh to withdrawe me.

到達我所管轄的豐裕的寶島；
　　何況，你還有摯友在為你關心。

從我教養你以來，你曾享受歡樂，
　　同時却有多少人遭到我的白眼！
難道你反而要對我訂下規約，
　　背叛你的主後，迫我聽你調遣？
你旣生於我這多變之國，不免
　　就得跟着衆人隨風飄零。
你與其自苦，不如多聽我的勸勉；
　　何况，你還有摯友在為你關心。

三　反駁幸運

我咒詛你的教義，一味與我為難。
　　盲目的女神，你休想劫奪我的摯友！
你使我結識了你手下的伙伴，
　　我感謝你。願你立將他們拘留！
他們所囤積的錢財在向你招手，
　　他們聚斂愈多，你愈好一手搗破；
好比疾病的前夕，必先削弱胃口：
　　這規律自可普遍應用，不會有錯。

幸運再辯

因爲我曾分贈給你一點財富，
　　如今我要收回，你便謾罵不已，
向我發洩怨氣，控我幻變無度。

Why sholdestow my realtee oppresse?
The see may ebbe and flowen more or lesse;
The welkne hath might to shyne, reyne, or hayle;
Right so mot I kythen my brotelnesse:
In general, this reule may nat fayle.

Lo, th'execucion of the majestee
That al purveyeth of his rightwysnesse,
That same thing "Fortune" clepen ye,
Ye blinde bestes, ful of lewednesse!
The hevene hath propretee of sikernesse,
This world hath ever resteles travayle;
Thy laste day is ende of myn intresse:
In general, this reule may nat fayle.

Lenvoy de Fortune

Princes, I prey you, of your gentilesse,
Lat nat this man on me thus crye and pleyne,
And I shal quyte you your bisinesse
At my requeste, as three of you or tweyne;
And, but you list releve him of his peyne,
Preyeth his beste frend, of his noblesse,
That to som beter estat he may atteyne.

你何苦污辱我的尊嚴,對我無禮?
豈不見海潮也有高低,忽落忽起;
　　風晴雨雪,天空也永在顛簸;
因此我也表現着這多變的定理:
　　這規律自可普遍應用,不會有錯。

要知道那統轄萬物的天父,
　　周覽宇宙,運用了公正大義,
而你們芸芸衆生,盲目的蠢物
　　竟認爲這就是"幸運"的標記!
其實天道雖然永恒不變,但大地
　　與人世,却奔逐漂忽,浮沉起落;
你這一生乃是我的興趣所寄:
　　這規律自可普遍應用,不會有錯。

幸運跋詞

公侯們哪,我求你們仁恕爲懷,
　　莫讓這個人對我不停地泣訴,
我請求你們趕快設法安排,
　　兩人或三人會商後予以照顧[1];
除非你們自願伸出一臂之助,
　　否則就請轉囑他的摯友輸財,
好使他踏上比較光明的道路。

　　　　　　　　　　　　方重譯

---

[1] 1390年,皇家賞賜臣民之權操縱於三位親王手中。

4 Moral Balade of Gentilesse

Geoffrey Chaucer

The firste stok, fader of gentilesse —
What man that claymeth gentil for to be
Must followe his trace, and alle his wittes dresse
Vertu to sewe, and vyces for to flee.
For unto vertu longeth dignitèe,
And noght the revers, saufly dar I deme,
Al were he mytre, croune, or diademe.

This firstè stok was ful of rightwisnesse,
Trewe of his word, sobre, pitous, and free,
Clene of his gost, and lovèd besinesse,
Ageinst the vyce of slouthe, in honestee;
And, but his heir love vertu, as dide he,
He is noght gentil, thogh he richè seme,
Al were he mytre, croune, or diademe.

Vyce may wel be heir to old richesse;
But ther may no man, as men may wel see,
Bequethe his heir his vertuous noblesse
That is appropred unto no degree,
But to the firstè fader in magestee,

四 高貴的品質
喬叟德頌

杰弗雷·喬叟

任何人若要自稱高貴超凡,
　　必須尊奉那品質崇高的始祖,
繼承他的遺志,他才是高貴之源,
　　後人應努力遵循美德,而消除
　　　敗行。原來有德才有榮,假如
行為不正,我敢肯定說,就一無可觀,
　　哪怕你戴上了法冠、皇冕或花環。

這位人類的始祖確是至德至善,
　　言而有信、沉靜、仁慈、寬厚待人、
心地純潔,且喜愛勤勞,厭惡懶散,
　　他認為勞動就是人的高尚本能;
　　　因此他的後裔,如果存心不仁,
即使金玉滿堂,却與高貴不相關,
　　哪怕你戴上了法冠、皇冕或花環。

世傳的財富往往造成後代的惡行;
　　而人們都可明了,那崇高的品質
却不能世代相承,貴冑的門庭
　　也沒有他們能獨佔的道德標飾,
　　　惟有始祖以德為貴,他的後世

That maketh him his heyre that can him queme,
Al were he mytre, croune, or diademe.

必須克勤克儉，以博取他的心歡，
哪怕你戴上了法冠、皇冕或花環。

方重譯

5 The Complaint of Chaucer to His Purse

Geoffrey Chaucer

To you, my purse, and to non other wight
Compleyne I, for ye be my lady dere!
I am so sory, now that ye be light,
That certés, but ye make me hevy chere,
Me were as leef be leyd upon my bere;
For which unto your mercy thus I crye:
Beth hevy again, or ellés mot I dye!

Now voucheth sauf this day, or it be night,
That I of yow the blisful soun may here,
Or see your colour, lik the sonné bright,
That of yelownesse hadde never pere.
Ye be my lif, ye be myn hertés stere,
Quene of comfòrt and of good companye:
Beeth hevy ageyne, or ellés mot I dye!

Now purse, that been to me my livés lyght
And saviour, as doun in this world here,
Out of this touné helpe me thurgh your might,

五　喬叟的怨詩致錢囊

杰弗雷・喬叟

我的錢囊，我要向你單獨地苦求，
　　惟有你才是我心愛的女郎！
你減輕了分量，眞叫我發愁；
　　我願你轉虧爲盈，飽滿、慈祥，
　　　　免得我窮途末路，走向死亡；
　　因此我要請你寬恩，向你討饒：
　　　　趕緊加重分量，否則我就完了！

求你在今天黑夜未臨以前，
　　讓我聽到你那幸福之音，
或是見到你的太陽般的容顏，
　　金黃閃爍，誰也不能同你競爭。
　　你是我的生命，惟你能駕馭我心，
你是慰藉之母，似應與我友好，
　　趕緊加重分量，否則我就完了！

錢囊呀，你照耀着我這生命之路，
　　在人世間惟有你是我的護神，
但是你旣不願爲我把守空庫，

　　怨詩爲喬叟早期慣用詩格，本詩是他的晚年作品，以錢囊代替一般怨詩中的女郎。本詩刊行後得亨利四世賞識，詩人於1399年10月3日獲皇家恩俸。

Syn that ye wol nat ben my tresorere;
For I am shave as nye as any frere.
But yet I pray unto your curtesie:
Beth hevy agen, or ellès mot I dye!

        Envoy [to Henry IV]

O conquerour of Brutès Albyon,
Which that by line and free eleccioùn
Been verray king, this song to you I sende;
And ye, that mowèn alle oure harmes amende,
Have minde upon my supplicacioùn!

就請你送我離去這座都城⑴；
　我囊空如洗，像個禿頭僧人。
我只有眞心誠意向你祈禱：
　趕緊加重分量，否則我就完了！

喬叟題跋

啊，我的君王，你威震英倫，
　人們一致擁護，王位世承，
你能清除我們心中憂鬱，
　讓我奉獻於你這首歌曲；
請你眷顧我這懇切的下情！

方重譯

⑴喬叟因生活窘迫，曾擬遷出倫敦。

6 Forget Not Yet
The Lover Beseecheth his Mistress not to Forget his Steadfast Faith and True Intent

Thomas Wyatt

Forget not yet the tried entent
Of such a truth as I have meant;
My great travail so gladly spent,
Forget not yet!

Forget not yet when first began
The weary life ye know, since whan
The suit, the service, none tell can;
Forget not yet!

Forget not yet the great assays,
The cruel wrong, the scornful ways,
The painful patience in delays,
Forget not yet!

Forget not, yet forget not this —
How long ago hath been, and is,

韋艾特(1503?—1542),年僅十二歲即在劍橋大學攻讀,以優異成績畢業。後任職宮廷,經常奉命出使歐洲各國。韋艾特把意大利首創的十四行詩體稍

六　別忘了

戀人祈求薄情女
別忘了他的眞心實意

托馬斯·韋艾特

別忘了我曾對你
懷有眞情，忠貞不渝；
苦苦追求，樂此不疲，
別忘了！

別忘了咱倆結識
在浮生厭倦之際；
從此迷戀你，殷勤無比，
別忘了！

別忘了我百般嘗試，
你却冷酷而鄙夷，
一味拖延；我則忍耐到底，
別忘了！

別忘了，別忘了一點——
我早已和你繾綣，

微改變韻律介紹到英國來，成爲伊麗莎白時期詩歌及戲劇的主要創作形式。韋艾特長於短篇抒情詩，多用白描手法抒寫。

The mind that never meant amiss —
Forget not yet!

Forget not then thine own approved,
The which so long hath thee so loved,
Whose steadfast faith yet never moved —
Forget not this!

如今癡心依然——
別忘了!

別忘了你曾默認
久久苦戀你的人;
信誓旦旦不變心——
別忘了!

孫梁譯

7 The Silent Lover

Walter Raleigh

Passions are liken'd best to floods and streams,
  The shallow murmur, but the deep are dumb;
So, when affection yields discourse, it seems
  The bottom is but shallow whence they come.
They that are rich in words, in words discover
That they are poor in that which makes a lover.

　　拉雷(1552?－1618)，英國文藝復興時代全面發
展人物，既是政治家，又是航海家，並且寫詩作曲。
詹姆士一世統治時期，拉雷奉命率領探險隊出海，後

七　沉默的戀人

華爾特・拉雷

流水比喻激情最妥，
　　淺水淙淙而深水無聲；
恰如情思倘若傾吐，
　　可知心底了無深情。
戀人如甜言蜜語，
　　骨子裏虛情假意。

孫梁譯

因外交糾紛，被處以極刑。詩作僅存約三十首，包括 *The Lie, Cynthia* 等。

8 Whilst It Is Prime

Edmund Spenser

Fresh Spring, the herald of loves mighty king,
In whose cote-armour richly are displayd
All sorts of flowers, the which on earth do spring,
In goodly colours gloriously arrayd —
Goe to my love, where she is carelesse layd,
Yet in her winters bowre not well awake;
Tell her the joyous time wil not be staid,
Unlesse she doe him by the forelock take;
Bid her therefore her selfe soone ready make,
To wayt on Love amongst his lovely crew;
Where every one, that misseth then her make,
Shall be by him amearst with penance dew.
    Make hast, therefore, sweet love, whilest it is prime;
    For none can call againe the passèd time.

斯賓塞(1552?—1599),生於倫敦,劍橋大學文學碩士。名作有《牧人歷本》(*The Shepheardes Calender*)、《仙后》(*The Faerie Queene*)。創造了獨特韻律 ababbcbcc 的"斯賓塞詩體"(Spen-

八 行樂當及時

埃特蒙·斯賓塞

清芬的春天傳訊:愛神君臨人間,
春光披上盛裝,盡情展示
大地茁生的百花鬥妍,
燦爛似錦,遍地華滋。
告訴我的情人——她依然安臥,
慵倦,冬眠不覺春曉;
告訴她:歡樂時光莫蹉跎,
良辰美景須趁早;
要她即刻梳粧整容,
充當俊美扈從,侍奉愛神;
神明將灑遍甘露,
撫慰渴望的衆生。
鍾愛的情人,行樂當及時;
春去也,無計喚住。

孫梁譯

---

serian stanza)。

《行樂當及時》選自斯賓塞於1591至1594年間創作的組詩《情詩小品》(*Amoretti*)。

9 Sweet Is the Rose

Edmund Spenser

Sweet is the Rose, but growes vpon a brere;
   sweet is the Iunipere, but sharpe his bough;
   sweet is the Eglantine, but pricketh nere;
   sweet is the firbloome, but his braunches rough.
Sweet is the Cypresse, but his rynd is tough,
   sweet is the nut, but bitter is his pill;
   sweet is the broome-flowre, but yet sowre enough;
   and sweet is Moly, but his root is ill.
So euery sweet with soure is tempred still,
   that maketh it be coueted the more:
   for easie things that may be got at will,
   most sorts of men doe set but little store.
Why then should I accoumpt of little paine,
   that endlesse pleasure shall vnto me gaine.

九　玫瑰多美呵

埃德蒙·斯賓塞

玫瑰多美呵，可每朵長刺；
杜松多美呵，可枝椏銳利；
野薔薇多美呵，可刺入嫩肌；
樅樹多美呵，可枝柯粗厲；
柏樹多美呵，可樹皮堅無比；
碩果多美呵，可果皮澀而苦；
金雀花多美呵，可酸得出奇；
牟荣花多美呵，可根兒爛到底。
甘美的萬物都混雜酸味，
　　却令人迷戀，如醉如癡；
凡是唾手可得的東西，
　　人們都棄之若敝屣；
我何不忍受細微苦痛，
終於能換來樂趣無窮?!

孫梁譯

10 A Ditty

Philip Sidney

My true-love hath my heart, and I have his,
By just exchange one for another given:
I hold his dear, and mine he cannot miss,
There never was a better bargain driven:
    My true-love hath my heart, and I have his.

His heart in me keeps him and me in one,
My heart in him his thoughts and senses guides:
He loves my heart, for once it was his own,
I cherish his because in me it bides:
    My true-love hath my heart, and I have his.

　　錫特尼（1554—1586），生於英國肯特郡，曾任外交官、議員、司令，於1586年聚特芬（Zutphen）戰役中受傷致死。著名作品包括收錄一百零八首十四行詩的《阿斯屈洛菲爾與絲丹拉》（*Astrophel and Stella*）、田園傳奇詩《阿凱廸亞》（*Arcadia*）、文

十　謠曲

菲力普・錫特尼

意中人佔有我的心，我佔了他的魂靈，
心心相印，一點靈犀；
我的心他不會失去，他的心是我的命，
世上再沒有更好的默契；
意中人佔有我的心，我佔了他的魂靈。

他的情意使咱倆一條心，
我的深情教他心思專一；
他愛我的心，因我對他一往情深，
我珍惜他的心，因他對我傾心；
意中人佔有我的心，我佔了他的魂靈。

宗白譯
孫梁校

藝論著《詩辯》（*The Defence of Poesie*）。
　　《謠曲》屬民謠體短詩，仿照法國古詩的回旋體（rondel），第五及第十行重複第一行，成爲叠句（refrain）；每行均爲五步抑揚格，但第二節中作變化，有破格及出韵。

11 Nature
   (Extracted from *Tamburlaine,* Pt. I, II, vii.)

Christopher Marlowe

Nature that framed us of four elements,
Warring within our breasts for regiment,
Doth teach us all to have aspiring minds:
Our souls, whose faculties can comprehend
The wondrous architecture of the world,
And measure every wandering planet's course,
Still climbing after knowledge infinite,
And always moving as the restless spheres,
Will us to wear ourselves and never rest,
Until we reach the ripest fruit of all.

馬羅（1564－1593），生於英國坎特伯雷。重要作品包括《帖木耳大帝》(*Tamburlaine the Great*)、《浮士德博士的悲劇》(*The Tragedy of Dr. Faustus*)、《馬耳他的猶太人》(*The Jew of Malta*)、

十一　大自然

（節譯自詩劇《帖木耳》；第一部，第二幕，第七場）

克利斯朵夫・馬羅

大自然賦予人四大元素(1)——
在內心衝突，爭着控制性靈；
造化啓廸衆生奮發而探索，
人的靈智能理解萬物：
領悟宇宙的神奇結構，
測量天體運行軌迹；
不斷追求無窮知識，
宛如星球生生不息；
性靈敦促我們鍥而不捨，
直到採摘豐碩的果實。

孫梁譯

《愛德華二世》（*Edward II*）等。
(1)四大元素是西方古代與中世紀的哲學概念，指土、氣、水、火；宇宙萬物（包括人類）均由這些元素組成。

12 The Passionate Shepherd to His Love

Christopher Marlowe

Come live with me and be my Love,
And we will all the pleasures prove
That hills and valleys, dale and field,
And all the craggy mountains yield.

There will we sit upon the rocks
And see the shepherds feed their flocks,
By shallow rivers, to whose falls
Melodious birds sing madrigals.

There will I make thee beds of roses
And a thousand fragrant posies,
A cap of flowers, and a kirtle
Embroider'd all with leaves of myrtle.

A gown made of the finest wool,
Which from our pretty lambs we pull,
Fair linéd slippers for the cold,
With buckles of the purest gold.

十二 熱烈的牧人情歌

克利斯朵夫・馬羅

做我伴侶吧永不分離；
青山綠野繞幽谿，
巍巍峯巒插雲霄，
賞心悅目多逍遙！

咱倆偎依岩石上，
觀賞牧童飼羣羊；
清溪潺潺脉脉流，
鳥鳴嚶嚶爲伴奏。

薔薇花，舖新床，
獻萬千花束芬芳；
戴花冠，披新裝，
編自翠葉桃金孃。(1)

純羊毛，製長袍，
採自嬌美小羊羔；
鑲邊繡鞋多輕巧，
純金扣子扣得牢。

《熱烈的牧人情歌》作於斯賓塞的《牧人歷本》之後，是英國文壇當時盛行的田園詩作品之一，通篇節奏輕快。

(1)一種植物，尤指愛神木。

A belt of straw and ivy buds
With coral clasps and amber studs:
And if these pleasures may thee move,
Come live with me and be my Love.

Thy silver dishes for thy meat
As precious as the gods do eat,
Shall on an ivory table be
Prepared each day for thee and me.

The shepherd swains shall dance and sing
For thy delight each May-morning:
If these delights thy mind may move,
Then live with me and be my Love.

珊瑚鈎,琥珀鈕,
麥杆青藤腰帶束;
要是這些你中意,
做我伴侶不分離。

銀杯盤,盛佳餚,
美味只供仙女曹;
象牙桌,擺得滿,
每日享用你與咱。

初夏清晨飽眼福:
牧人風流載歌舞;
要是這些你中意,
做我伴侶吧永不分離。

孫梁譯

13 Shall I Compare Thee to a Summer's Day (XVIII)

William Shakespeare

Shall I compare thee to a summer's day?
Thou art more lovely and more temperate.
Rough winds do shake the darling buds of May,
And summer's lease hath all too short a date:
Sometimes too hot the eye of heaven shines,
And often is his gold complexion dimmed;
And every fair from fair sometime declines,
By chance, or nature's changing course, untrimmed:
But thy eternal summer shall not fade,
Nor lose possession of that fair thou owest;
Nor shall Death brag thou wanderest in his shade
When in eternal lines to time thou growest.
  So long as men can breathe or eyes can see,
  So long lives this, and this gives life to thee.

    威廉・莎士比亞（1564—1616），生於英國斯特拉特福鎮，一生創作了三十七部戲劇、一百五十四首十四行詩、兩首長詩和其他詩歌。著名劇作包括《馴悍記》(*Taming of the Shrew*)、《羅密歐與朱麗葉》(*Romeo and Juliet*)、《哈姆雷特》(*Hamlet*)等。

    莎士比亞的十四行詩大部份獻給一位貴族青年，其餘二十多篇的對象則是一位"黑膚女士"（the dark lady）；莎士比亞主要用五步抑揚格（iambic pentameter），韵律是 abab，cdcd，efef，gg。本書收錄其

十三　能否把你比作夏日璀璨

（第十八首）

威廉·莎士比亞

能否把你比作夏日璀璨？
你却比炎夏更可愛溫存；
狂風摧殘五月花蕊嬌姸，
夏天匆匆離去毫不停頓。
蒼天明眸(1)有時過於灼熱，
金色臉容往往蒙上陰翳；
一切優美形象不免褪色(2)，
偶然摧折或自然地老去(3)。
而你如仲夏繁茂不凋謝，
秀雅風姿將永遠翩翩(4)；
死神無法逼你氣息奄奄，
你將永生於不朽詩篇。
　　只要人能呼吸眼不盲，
　　這詩和你將千秋流芳。

孫梁譯

中六首。
(1) 指太陽。
(2) 原句中第一個fair是普通名詞，指具體的美的形象，第二個fair是抽象名詞，指美貌、優美等。
(3) 原句中untrimmed原意爲"剝掉（美觀的衣服等）"，此處隱喻"奪去（美貌等）"。
(4) 原句的owest等於現代英語的own，意爲"所有"或"擁有"。

14 When in Disgrace with Fortune and Men's Eyes (XXIX)

William Shakespeare

When in disgrace with fortune and men's eyes,
I all alone beweep my outcast state,
And trouble deaf heaven with my bootless cries,
And look upon myself, and curse my fate,
Wishing me like to one more rich in hope,
Featured like him, like him with friends possess'd,
Desiring this man's art, and that man's scope,
With what I most enjoy contented least;
Yet in these thoughts myself almost despising,
Haply I think on thee, — and then my state
(Like to the lark at break of day arising
From sullen earth) sings hymns at heaven's gate;
    For thy sweet love remember'd, such wealth brings,
    That then I scorn to change my state with kings.

十四　可嘆時運不濟衆人唾棄

（第二十九首）

威廉・莎士比亞

可嘆時運不濟衆人唾棄，
爲飄零人間而獨自哭泣；
怨蒼天不聞兮徒然呼籲，
顧影自憐兮咒命運殘酷；
願自己如他人前程似錦，
或儀表堂堂或高朋滿座，
有此人的機緣那人的本領(1)，
對自己的長處却不滿足；
一味自怨自艾自暴自棄，
但偶爾想到你便如雲雀(2)，
於拂曉時從陰霾的大地
飛向雲間天堂高歌不息；

　　　回憶你的情愫如獲寶藏，
　　　寧願困厄不屑南面稱王。

孫梁譯

---

(1)原句中art用本義"技能、本領"；scope意爲良機，左右逢源，或博學多才。

(2)原句中haply等於it happens或by chance（偶然，碰巧）。

15 When to the Sessions of Sweet Silent Thought (XXX)

William Shakespeare

When to the sessions of sweet silent thought
I summon up remembrance of things past,
I sigh the lack of many a thing I sought,
And with old woes new wail my dear time's waste:
Then can I drown an eye, unused to flow,
For precious friends hid in death's dateless night,
And weep afresh love's long-since cancell'd woe,
And moan the expense of many a vanish'd sight.
Then can I grieve at grievances foregone,
And heavily from woe to woe tell o'er
The sad account of fore-bemoaned moan,
Which I new pay as if not paid before.
 But if the while I think on thee, dear friend,
 All losses are restored, and sorrows end.

---

(1) 原句中 sessions 及 summon up 均為法律術語，意為"開庭，審理"及"傳令（出庭）"。

開端四行中有不少嘶音（sibilant），如〔s〕、〔z〕〔ʃ〕、〔θ〕等；尤其用〔s〕押 sessions, sweet, silent 三詞的頭韵，均以迂緩細微的聲調曲傳沉思

十五　在寧謐的沉思中憶往昔

（第三十首）

威廉·莎士比亞

在寧謐的沉思中憶往昔，
如法官鞫審時——傳訊(1)；
為無數企冀成泡影而嘆息，
舊恨生新愁，虛度好光陰；
念摯友長眠黃泉無盡期，
乾涸的眼中不禁涕泗流；
縱然愛情的痛苦早忘記，
昔日情景(2)似烟雲；又悲愁，
為消逝的哀怨再度惆悵，
把一樁樁沉痛往事數遍(3)；
以往的嗚咽又刻骨嚙腸，
猶如償還積欠的孽債；
　然而一想起你，親愛的人，
　一切損失抵銷，不再消沉。

孫梁譯

冥想的情懷。
(2)某些注釋者認為這裏的sight應為sigh（嘆息）。
(3)原句中tell o'er等於tell over，跟下一句中的account及pay均為財務用語，可見莎翁善用世俗事務的詞語。

16 Not Marble, Not the Gilded Monuments (LV)

William Shakespeare

Not marble, not the gilded monuments
Of princes, shall outlive this powerful rhyme;
But you shall shine more bright in these contents
Than unswept stone, besmeared with sluttish time.
When wasteful war shall statues overturn,
And broils root out the work of masonry,
Nor Mars his sword nor war's quick fire shall burn
The living record of your memory.
'Gainst death and all-oblivious enmity
Shall you pace forth; your praise shall still find room,
Even in the eyes of all posterity
That wear this world out to the ending doom.
  So, till the judgment that yourself arise,
    You live in this, and dwell in lovers' eyes.

十六　沒有雲石或王公們金的墓碑

（第五十五首）

威廉·莎士比亞

沒有雲石或王公們金的墓碑
能夠和我這些強勁的詩比壽；
你將永遠閃耀於這些詩篇裏，
遠勝過那被時光塗髒的石頭。
當着殘暴的戰爭把銅像推翻，
或內訌把城池蕩成一片廢墟，
無論戰神的劍或戰爭的烈焰
都毀不掉你的遺芳的活歷史。
突破死亡和湮沒一切的仇恨，
你將昂然站起來；對你的讚美
將在萬世萬代的眼睛裏彪炳，
直到這世界消耗完了的末日。
　　這樣，直到最後審判把你喚醒，
　　你長在詩裏和情人眼裏輝映。

梁宗岱譯

17 Since Brass, nor Stone, nor Earth, nor Boundless Sea (LXV)

William Shakespeare

Since brass, nor stone, nor earth, nor boundless sea,
But sad mortality o'ersways their power,
How with this rage shall beauty hold a plea,
Whose action is no stronger than a flower?
Oh, how shall summer's honey breath hold out
Against the wreckful siege of battering days,
When rocks impregnable are not so stout,
Nor gates of steel so strong, but Time decays?
Oh fearful meditation! where, alack!
Shall Time's best jewel from Time's chest lie hid?
Or what strong hand can hold his swift foot back?
Or who his spoil of beauty can forbid?
    Oh none, unless this miracle have might,
    That in black ink my love may still shine bright.

十七　既然是鐵石，大地，無邊的海洋

（第六十五首）

威廉·莎士比亞

既然是鐵石，大地，無邊的海洋，
儘管堅強也不抵無常一霸，
美貌又怎能控訴他這種猖狂，
論力量自己還只抵一朵嬌花？
啊，夏天的芬芳怎能抵得了
猛衝的光陰摧枯拉朽的圍攻。
既然是儘管頑強的石壁有多牢，
鐵門有多硬，也會給時間爛通？
可怕的想法啊！時間的瓌寶，唉，
要藏到哪裏纔免進時間的無底櫃？
哪隻手纔能拖住他飛毛腿跑不來？
誰能攔阻他把美貌一下子摧毀？
誰也不能，除非有法寶通靈：
我的愛能在墨痕裏永放光明。

卞之琳譯

18 When in the Chronicle of Wasted Time (CVI)

William Shakespeare

When in the chronicle of wasted time
I see descriptions of the fairest wights,
And beauty making beautiful old rhyme,
In praise of ladies dead, and lovely knights,
Then in the blazon of sweet beauty's best,
Of hand, of foot, of lip, of eye, of brow,
I see their antique pen would have express'd
Even such a beauty as you master now.
So all their praises are but prophecies
Of this our time, all you prefiguring;
And, for they look'd but with divining eyes,
They had not skill enough your worth to sing:
    For we, which now behold these present days,
    Have eyes to wonder, but lack tongues to praise.

十八 過往世代的記載裏常常見到
（第一○六首）

威廉·莎士比亞

過往世代的記載裏常常見到
前人把最俊俏人物描摹盡致，
美貌如何使古老的詩句也美妙，
配得上歌頌美女和風流騎士，
看人家誇讚美貌是怎樣的無比，
什麼手，什麼脚，什麼嘴，什麼眼，什麼眉，
我總是看出來他們古雅的手筆
差不多恰好表現了你的秀美。
所以他們的讚辭都無非是預言
我們這時代，都把你預先描畫；
他們却只用猜度的眼睛來觀看，
還不夠有本領歌唱你的眞價：
我們呢，親眼看到了今天的風光，
眼睛會驚訝，舌頭却不會頌揚。

卞之琳譯

19 Spring

Thomas Nashe

Spring, the sweet Spring, is the year's pleasant king;
Then blooms each thing, then maids dance in a ring,
Cold doth not sting, the pretty birds do sing,
　　Cuckoo, jug-jug, pu-we, to-witta-woo!

The palm and may make country houses gay,
Lambs frisk and play, the shepherds pipe all day,
And we hear aye birds tune this merry lay,
　　Cuckoo, jug-jug, pu-we, to-witta-woo!

The fields breathe sweet, the daisies kiss our feet,
Young lovers meet, old wives a-sunning sit,
In every street these tunes our ears do greet,
　　Cuckoo, jug-jug, pu-we, to-witta-woo!
　　Spring! the sweet Spring!

　　納希 (1567—1601),伊麗莎白時期 "大學才子"
之一,作品有傳奇小說《杰克‧威爾頓》(*The Life
of Jack Wilton*) 等。
　　《春天》一詩選自納希為宮廷娛樂所作的喜劇《維
爾‧塞默的遺言》(*Will Summer's Testament*),韻

十九　春

托馬斯·納希

春，甘美之春，一年之中的堯舜，
處處都有花樹，都有女兒環舞，
微寒但覺清和，佳禽爭着唱歌，
　嘔嘔，啾啾，哥哥，割麥、插一禾！

榆柳呀山楂，打扮着田舍人家，
羊羔嬉游，牧笛兒整日價吹奏，
百鳥總在和鳴，一片悠揚聲韵，
　嘔嘔，啾啾，哥哥，割麥、插一禾！

郊原蕩漾香風，雛菊吻人脚踵，
情侶作對成雙，老嫗坐曬陽光，
走向任何通衢，都有歌聲悅耳，
　嘔嘔，啾啾，哥哥，割麥、插一禾！
　春！甘美之春！

郭沫若譯

律主要是五步抑揚格，韵式是aaab，cccb，dddb，三節最後一行是叠句（refrain）；每節中除末一行外，其他三行都用腹韵（leonine rhyme），即第二音步的第二個詞同第五音步末尾的詞協韵。

20 Death Be Not Proud

Holy Sonnets: Divine Meditations 6

John Donne

Death be not proud, though some have called thee
Mighty and dreadfull, for, thou art not soe,
For, those, whom thou think'st, thou dost overthrow,
Die not, poore death, nor yet canst thou kill mee;
From rest and sleepe, which but thy pictures bee,
Much pleasure, then from thee, much more must flow,
And soonest our best men with thee doe goe,
Rest of their bones, and soules deliverie.
Thou art slave to Fate, chance, kings, and desperate men,
And dost with poyson, warre, and sicknesse dwell,
And poppie, or charmes can make us sleepe as well,
And better than thy stroake; why swell'st thou then?
One short sleepe past, wee wake eternally,
And death shall be no more, Death thou shalt die.

鄧恩（1573—1631），生於倫敦，就學於牛津、劍橋大學，1621年出任聖保羅大教堂教長，直至逝世。他的作品注重說理、議論和爭辯，與傳統婉約寫景的抒情詩歌大不相同，被稱為"玄學派詩人"（the

二十　死神莫驕妄

神聖的十四行詩：聖潔的沉思，第六首

約翰・鄧恩

死神莫驕妄，雖有人稱你
蠻橫可怖，其實外強中乾；
你自以爲能把衆生摧殘，
但枉然；可憐的死神，我超越你！
你不過類似睡眠、憩息，
必然比安眠更令人舒坦；
故而人傑英豪不怕歸天，
無非白骨入土，靈魂安息。
你受厄運、殺機、暴君與狂徒差遣，
用毒藥、戰爭和疾病害人；
鴉片與妖術也能使人昏，
且更靈驗，你何必如此氣焰?!
凡人了却浮生，但精神永生，
超脫死的魔掌，滅絕死神！

孫梁譯

---

metaphysical poets）。

《死神莫驕妄》一詩，格律不同於莎士比亞的十四行詩。首三節按abba韻律，結尾則用偶句，兩行協韻。

21 An Anatomie of the World
The First Anniversary (Extract)

John Donne

Wee are borne ruinous: poore mothers cry,
That children come not right, nor orderly;
Except they headlong come and fall upon
An ominous precipitation.
How witty's ruine! how importunate
Upon mankinde! it labour'd to frustrate
Even Gods purpose; and made woman, sent
For mans reliefe, cause of his languishment.
They were to good ends, and they are so still,
But accessory, and principall in ill;
For that first marriage was our funerall:
One woman at one blow, then kill'd us all,
And singly, one by one, they kill us now.
We doe delightfully our selves allow
To that consumption; and profusely blinde,
Wee kill our selves to propagate our kinde.
...

　　《塵世剖析》是應制之作，爲羅伯特‧德魯雷爵士（Sir Robert Druary）之亡女伊麗莎白而寫；約翰‧鄧恩借題發揮，表現他對人類世界的悲觀絕望。選譯之兩節，通篇用偶句，每兩行協韵。

二十一　塵世剖析
——周年悼詩（節選）

約翰·鄧恩

毀滅與生俱來：母親們悲嘆
兒女生不逢辰，却爭着投胎，
橫衝直撞地奔向人間，
只落得頭破血流多慘。
毀滅神通廣大[1]，人類受盡煎熬！
擾得神都昏瞶：使淑女窈窕
降生人寰，理應撫慰男子，
却播弄他——迷得如醉如痴。
她們假惺惺，似乎一貫和善，
實則禍水，興風作浪，推波助瀾；
原來始祖婚禮乃是衆人葬儀，
一個女人造孽，結果害死全體[2]；
如今變換手法，男子逐個被殺。
我們却甘心情願受欺壓
而泯滅；盲目得近乎荒唐，
自戕而生育，害子孫遭殃。
……

---

[1] 原句中形容詞witty由名詞wit派生，依wit的本義作"富於才智的"解。

[2] 指《聖經》所載：人類始祖亞當與夏娃食禁果，結爲夫婦，造成人間苦難。

Shee, shee is dead; shee's dead: when thou knowest this,
Thou knowest how poore a trifling thing man is.
And learn'st thus much by our Anatomie,
The heart being perish'd, no part can be free.
And that except thou feed (not banquet) on
The supernaturall food, Religion,
Thy better Growth growes withered, and scant;
Be more then man, or thou'rt lesse then an Ant.
Then, as mankinde, so is the worlds whole frame
Quite out of joynt, almost created lame:
For, before God had made up all the rest,
Corruption entred, and deprav'd the best:
It seis'd the Angels, and then first of all
The world did in her cradle take a fall,
And turn'd her braines, and tooke a generall maime,
Wronging each joynt of th'universall frame.
The noblest part, man, felt it first; and than
Both beasts and plants, curst in the curse of man.
So did the world from the first houre decay,
That evening was beginning of the day,
And now the Springs and Sommers which we see,
Like sonnes of women after fiftie bee.
And new Philosophy calls all in doubt,

她棄世,她棄世了;得噩耗
便悟到:人是多麼渺小。
吟誦本篇剖析應領會:
一旦心碎,靈肉俱毀。
除非你篤信宗教,
吸取營養不過飽,
聖潔心靈將萎靡;
超脫紅塵,否則不如豸蟻。
芸芸衆生,大千世界,
均支離破碎,幾乎天生殘廢;
上帝創造塵世之前,
腐敗已生根,甚至腐蝕聖賢,
神仙都不免;故而開天闢地,
世界形成之際便傾圮,
一團混亂,一片混沌,
茫茫宇宙均迷濛;
萬物之靈首先觸景生愁,
人的厄運波及草木禽獸。
因此宇宙洪荒即腐朽,
白晝黑夜顛倒令人憂;
陽春炎夏應繁盛,
却似年過半百衰翁。
新思潮懷疑一切(1),

---

(1)指當時反封建、反宗教的人文主義新思潮,以及哥白尼倡導的近代天文學等。

The Element of fire is quite put out;
The Sun is lost, and th'earth, and no mans wit
Can well direct him where to looke for it.
And freely men confesse that this world's spent,
When in the Planets, and the Firmament
They seeke so many new; they see that this
Is crumbled out againe to his Atomies.
'Tis all in peeces, all cohaerence gone;

. . .

心靈的聖火熄滅;
陽光慘淡,大地陰沉,
人的智慧非指路明燈。
人類探索太空天體,
一心追求萬千新奇;
却只見萬物分崩離析,
於是衆生憬悟世界末日。
一切破碎,了無理性邏輯;
……

孫梁譯

22 To the Memory of My Beloved, the Author Mr. William Shakespeare And What He Hath Left Us

Ben Jonson

To draw no envy, *Shakespeare*, on thy name,
   Am I thus ample to thy book and fame;
While I confess thy writings to be such
   As neither *man* nor *Muse* can praise too much.
'Tis true, and all men's suffrage. But these ways
   Were not the paths I meant unto thy praise:
For silliest ignorance on these may light,
   Which, when it sounds at best, but echoes right;
Or blind affection, which doth ne'er advance
   The truth, but gropes, and urgeth all by chance;
Or crafty malice might pretend this praise,
   And thinke to ruin, where it seemed to raise.
These are, as some infamous bawd or whore
   Should praise a matron. What could hurt her more?
But thou art proof against them, and, indeed
   Above th' ill fortune of them, or the need.
I therefore will begin. Soul of the age!

二十二　題威廉‧莎士比亞先生的遺著，紀念吾敬愛的作者

本‧瓊生

莎士比亞，不是想給你的名字招嫉妒，
我這樣竭力讚揚你的人和書；
說你的作品簡直是超凡入聖，
人和詩神怎樣誇也不會過份。
這是實情，誰也不可能有異議。
我本來可不想用這種辦法來稱道你，
生怕給可憐的"無知"開方便之門
（它講得像挺好，實際是人云亦云），
也怕讓盲目的"偏愛"隨意搬弄
（它從不講真實，只瞎摸亂捧），
也怕叫奸詐的"惡意"撿起來耍花招．
（它存心譭謗，因此就故意抬高）。
這就像娼門誇獎了良家婦女，
還有什麼比這個更大的揶揄？
可是你經得起這一套，既不稀罕，
也不怕它們帶給你什麼災難。
因此我可以開言。時代的靈魂！

　　瓊生（1573？—1637），生於英國威斯敏斯特，莎士比亞的朋友。作品有戲劇十八部（其中有少數未完成，也不包括與其他作家合作的劇本）、《森林》詩集、《灌木》詩集。

The applause! delight! the wonder of our stage!
My *Shakespeare*, rise; I will not lodge thee by
 Chaucer, or *Spenser,* or bid *Beaumont* lie
A little further, to make thee a room;
 Thou art a monument without a tomb,
And art alive still while thy book doth live,
 And we have wits to read and praise to give.
That I not mix thee so, my brain excuses,
 I mean with great, but disproportioned *Muses*;
For, if I thought my iudgement were of yeeres,
 I should commit thee surely with thy peeres,
And tell, how farre thou didst our *Lily* out-shine,
 Or sporting *Kid,* or *Marlowes* mighty line.
And though thou hadst small *Latine,* and less *Greeke,*
 From thence to honour thee, I would not seeke
For names; but call forth thund'ring *Æschilus,*
 Euripides, and *Sophocles* to vs,
Paccuuius, Accius, him of *Cordoua* dead,

---

(1)威廉·巴斯（William Basse）寫過一首詩《挽莎士比亞》，開頭幾行說："著名的斯賓塞，你靠博學的喬叟躺過去一點，稀有的卜蒙，你靠斯賓塞躺過去一點，給莎士比亞在你們三重的陵墓裏騰出個鋪位。"本·瓊生這裏針對了這幾句話。卜蒙（Francis Beaumont, 1584－1616），莎士比亞同時代戲劇家。

(2)黎里（John Lyly, 1554？－1606），基德（Thomas

我們所擊節稱賞的戲劇元勛！
我的莎士比亞，起來吧；我不想安置你
在喬叟、斯賓塞身邊，卜蒙也不必
躺開一點兒，給你騰出個鋪位⑴：
你是不需要陵墓的一個紀念碑，
你還是活着的，只要你的書還在，
只要我們會讀書，會說出好歹。
我還有頭腦，不把你如此相混——
同那些偉大而不相稱的詩才並論：
因爲我如果認爲要按年代評判，
那當然就必須扯上你同輩的伙伴，
指出你怎樣蓋過了我們的黎里
淘氣的基德、馬羅⑵的雄偉的筆力。
儘管你不大懂拉丁，更不通希臘文，
我不到別處去找名字來把你推尊：
我要喚起雷鳴的埃斯庫羅斯，
還有歐里庇得斯、索福克利斯、
巴古維烏斯、阿修斯⑶、科多巴詩才⑷，

Kid, 1558—94），馬羅（Christopher Marlow, 1564—93）都是莎士比亞同時代而稍早的戲劇家，對莎士比亞有過影響。

⑶巴古維烏斯（Paccuvius, 公元前220？—132），阿修斯（Accius, 公元前170？—90？）都是羅馬悲劇家。

⑷"科多巴詩才"指羅馬悲劇家塞內加（Seneca, 公元前4？—公元65），生於西班牙科多巴城。

To life againe, to heare thy Buskin tread,
And shake a Stage: Or, when thy Sockes were on,
    Leaue thee alone, for the comparison
Of all, that insolent *Greece,* or haughtie *Rome*
    Sent forth, or since did from their ashes come.
Triúmph, my *Britaine,* thou hast one to showe,
    To whom all Scenes of *Europe* homage owe.
He was not of an age, but for all time!
    And all the *Muses* still were in their prime,
When like *Apollo* he came forth to warme
    Our eares, or like a *Mercury* to charme!
Nature her selfe was proud of his designes,
    And ioy'd to weare the dressing of his lines!
Which were so richly spun, and wouen so fit,
    As, since, she will vouchsafe no other Wit.
The merry *Greeke,* tart *Aristophanes,*
    Neat *Terence,* witty *Plautus,* now not please;
But antiquated, and deserted lye
    As they were not of Natures family.
Yet must I not giue Nature all: Thy Art,
    My gentle *Shakespeare,* must enioy a part.
For though the *Poets* matter, Nature be,
    His Art doth giue the fashion. And, that he,
Who casts to write a liuing line, must sweat,

---

(1)當時悲劇角色穿半統靴,喜劇角色穿輕履,習慣以"半統靴"代表悲劇,"輕履"代表喜劇。

(2)太陽神阿波羅也是音樂神,神使邁克利善於詞令。

也喚回人世來,聽你的半統靴登台,
震動劇壇:要是你穿上了輕履(1),
就讓你獨自去和他們全體來比一比——
不管是驕希臘傲羅馬送來的先輩
或者是他們的灰燼裏出來的後代。
得意吧,我的不列顛,你拿得出一個人,
他可以折服歐羅巴全部的戲文。
他不屬於一個時代而屬於所有的世紀!
所有的詩才都還在全盛時期,
他出來就像阿波羅聳動了聽聞,
或者像邁克利顛倒了我們的神魂(2)。
天籟本身以他的心裁而得意,
穿起他的詩句來好不歡喜!
它們是織得多富麗,縫得多合適!
從此她不願叫別的才子來裁製。
輕鬆的希臘人,尖刻的阿里斯托芬,
俐落的泰棱斯,機智的普勞塔斯(3),到如今
索然無味了,陳舊了,冷清清上了架,
都因為他們並不是天籟世家。
然而我決不把一切歸之於天成:
溫柔的莎士比亞,你的工夫也有份。
雖說自然就是詩人的材料,
還是靠人工產生形體。誰想要
鑄煉出你筆下那樣的活生生一句話,

---

(3)泰棱斯(Terence, 公元前185-159),普勞塔斯
(Plautus, 公元前254?-184),都是羅馬喜劇家。

(Such as thine are) and strike the second heat
Vpon the *Muses* anuile: turne the same,
   (And himselfe with it) that he thinkes to frame;
Or for the lawrell, he may gaine a scorne,
   For a good *Poet's* made, as well as borne.
And such wert thou. Looke how the fathers face
   Liues in his issue, euen so, the race
Of *Shakespeares* minde, and manners brightly shines
   In his well torned, and true-filed lines:
In each of which, he seemes to shake a Lance,
   As brandish't at the eyes of Ignorance.
Sweet Swan of *Auon!* what a sight it were
   To see thee in our waters yet appeare,
And make those flights vpon the bankes of *Thames,*
   That so did take *Eliza,* and our *Iames!*
But stay, I see thee in the *Hemisphere*
   Aduanc'd, and made a Constellation there!
Shine forth, thou Starre of *Poets,* and with rage,
   Or influence, chide, or cheere the drooping Stage;
Which, since thy flight from hence, hath mourn'd like night,
   And despaires day, but for thy Volumes light.

---

(1) "莎士比亞"的姓氏由"揮"（Shake）"槍"（Speare）二字拼成，本‧瓊生在這裏開了一個玩笑。

(2) 阿文河是莎士比亞家鄉的河流。

就必須流汗,必須再燒紅,再錘打,
緊貼着詩神的鐵砧,連人帶件,
扳過來拗過去,為了叫形隨意轉;
要不然桂冠不上頭,笑罵落一身,
因為好詩人靠天生也是靠煉成。
你就是這樣。常見到父親的面容
活在子女的身上,與此相同,
在他精雕細琢的字裏行間,
莎士比亞心性的兒孫光輝燦爛:
他寫一句詩就像揮一枝長槍(1),
朝着"無知"的眼睛不留情一晃!
阿文河(2)可愛的天鵝!該多麼好看,
如果你再在我們的水面上出現,
再飛臨泰晤士河崖(3),想當年就這樣
博得過伊麗莎(4)詹姆士陛下(5)的激賞!
可是別動吧,我看見你已經高升,
就在天庭上變成了一座星辰!
照耀吧,詩人界泰斗,或隱或顯,
申斥或鼓舞我們衰落的劇壇;
自從你高飛了,它就像黑夜般淒涼,
盼不到白晝,要沒有你大著放光。

卞之琳譯

―――――――

(3)當時倫敦戲院都在泰晤士河南岸。
(4)即伊麗莎白女王。
(5)即詹姆士一世。

23 To the Virgins, to Make Much of Time

Robert Herrick

Gather ye rose-buds while ye may,
   Old Time is still a-flying:
And this same flower that smiles today,
   Tomorrow will be dying.

The glorious lamp of heaven, the Sun,
   The higher he's a-getting,
The sooner will his race be run,
   And nearer he's to setting.

That age is best which is the first,
   When youth and blood are warmer;
But being spent, the worse, and worst
   Times, still succeed the former.

Then be not coy, but use your time;
   And while ye may, go marry:
For having lost but once your prime,
   You may for ever tarry.

二十三 勸女于歸

羅伯特·海立克

采采薔薇,及其未萎;
日月其邁,韶華如飛;
今夕此花,灼灼其姿;
翌日何如,將作枯枝。

朝暾炘炘,爛若天燈;
其光熠熠,載耀載昇;
彌迅其行,彌短其程;
日中必昃,言曛言暝。

年當荳蔻,妙齡之佳;
精血方盛,及春歲華。
一旦虛度,將自怨嗟;
韶光如駒,爰征以遐。

汝莫佯羞,及花仍稠,
采之擷之,覓一良儔。
韶華易逝,歲月難留;
良辰一誤,永無好逑。

吳漢文譯
孫　梁校

海立克(1591－1674),三十六歲時以國教教士身份佈道,同時勤奮寫詩,直至逝世。1648年出版詩集《金蘋果園》(*Hesperides*),共收詩作一千多首。

24 On His Deceased Wife

John Milton

Me thought I saw my late espoused Saint
  Brought to me like Alcestis from the grave,
  Whom Joves great Son to her glad Husband gave,
  Rescu'd from death by force though pale and faint,
Mine as whom washt from spot of child-bed taint,
  Purification in the old Law did save,
  And such, as yet once more I trust to have
  Full sight of her in Heaven without restraint,
Came vested all in white, pure as her mind:
  Her face was vail'd, yet to my fancied sight,
  Love, sweetness, goodness, in her person shin'd
So clear, as in no face with more delight.
  But O as to embrace me she enclin'd
  I wak'd, she fled, and day brought back my night.

　　彌爾頓（1608—1674），生於倫敦，畢業於劍橋大學。早期作品包括一些用拉丁文、希臘文和意大利文寫的短詩。晚年雙目失明。重要作品有長詩三篇：《失樂園》(*Paradise Lost*)、《復樂園》(*Paradise Regained*)、《力士參孫》(*Samson Agonistes*)。

　　《夢亡妻》為紀念1658年逝世的第二位妻子凱撒琳‧伍德考克(Catherine Woodcock)而寫。但也有人

二十四　夢亡妻

約翰・彌爾頓

我彷彿看見我最近死去的愛妻，
　　被送回人間，像赫克里斯當初，
　　從死亡手裏搶救的亞爾塞斯蒂⑴，
　　蒼白無力，又還給她的丈夫。
她好像古時洗身禮拯救的婦女，
　　已洗滌乾淨原來產褥的血污；
　　她穿着她心地那樣純淨的白衣，
　　正如我相信我會無拘無束
有一天在天堂裏面遇見她那樣。
　　她雖然蒙着面紗，我好像看見
　　她全身透出親熱、淑善和溫純，
比任何人臉上顯露的都叫人喜歡。
　　但她正俯身要和我擁抱時，我醒了，
　　人空了，白天帶來了黑夜漫漫。

殷寶書譯

說，這首詩指的是第一個太太瑪麗・鮑威爾（Mary Powell）。

⑴亞爾塞斯蒂（Alcestis）是埃達米塔斯（Admetus）的妻子，爲免丈夫死亡，她願意代死。她剛剛死了，赫克里斯就趕來營救；他與死神決鬥，並把亞爾塞斯蒂又奪回陽間。

25 To Cyriack Skinner

John Milton

Cyriack, this three years' day these eyes, though clear
    To outward view, of blemish or of spot,
    Bereft of light, their seeing have forgot;
    Nor to their idle orbs doth sight appear
Of sun or moon or star throughout the year,
    Or man or woman. Yet I argue not
    Against Heaven's hand or will, nor bate a jot
    Of heart or hope, but still bear up and steer
Right onward. What supports me, dost thou ask?
    The conscience, friend, to have lost them overplied
    In liberty's defense, my noble task,
Of which all Europe talks from side to side.
    This thought might lead me through the world's vain mask
    Content, though blind, had I no better guide.

西里亞克·斯基納是彌爾頓的學生，也是朋友。關於這首詩的創作背景，略述如下：查理第二逃亡到法國，收買歐洲的最大學者沙爾曼修，寫文章擁護王

二十五　給西里亞克·斯基納

約翰·彌爾頓

西里亞克呀，這三年中，我這雙眼，
　　從外表看來，似乎可以避免接觸污點，
　　什麼都看不見，久已失去了光明，
　　一年到頭不見太陽，月亮或星星，
無論男人女人，都不在我這等閒的眼中現形。
　　可是我並不埋怨上天的手段或用心，
　　我一點也沒有減少我的希望和熱情；
　　我仍舊要向上，向前邁進。
你要問這是什麼在支持我嗎？朋友，
　　那是道義呀，我為了保衛自由而失明，
　　保衛自由，這是我崇高的職務，
全歐羅巴到處都以這事為談話的中心。
　　這個思想引導我穿透世界的假面具，
　　我雖然瞎了也滿意，我有了無上的指針。

朱維之譯

權而痛罵英共和國。當時彌爾頓的一隻眼睛已瞎，醫生警告他，若再不休息，將要雙目成盲，但他還是不顧失明的威脅，與沙爾曼修筆戰。

26 On His Blindness

John Milton

When I consider how my light is spent
   Ere half my days, in this dark world and wide,
   And that one talent which is death to hide,
   Lodged with me useless, though my soul more bent
To serve therewith my Maker, and present
   My true account, lest He returning chide;
   "Doth God exact day-labor, light denied?"
   I fondly ask. But Patience, to prevent
That murmur, soon replies, "God doth not need
   Either man's work or his own gifts, who best
   Bear His mild yoke, they serve him best. His state
Is kingly: thousands at His bidding speed,
   And post o'er land and ocean without rest;
   They also serve who only stand and wait."

二十六 關於他的瞎眼

約翰·彌爾頓

我思量,我怎麼還未到生命的中途(1),
　　就已耗盡光明,走上這黑暗的,茫茫的世路,
　　我這完全埋沒了的庸才(2),對我毫無用處,
　　雖然我的心總是想要多多服務,
想要鞠躬盡瘁地服務於我的創造主,
　　算清我的賬,免得他要向我發怒;
　　"難道上帝不給光明却要計算日工嗎?"
　　我愚蠢地一問,"忍耐"就把我的話止住,
立刻回答道:"上帝不需要人的服務,
　　也不要你還給他什麼禮物;
　　誰能忍受得起痛苦,就是最好的服務:
他的國度氣派堂皇,聽他派遣的,不計其數,
　　他們奔走忙碌於海洋和大陸;
　　那些站立得穩,堅定不移的也是服務。"

朱維之譯

---

(1)彌爾頓在1652年失明,年四十四歲。
(2)"庸才"原文是"One talent",直譯為"一千銀子"。《馬太福音》第二十五章說一個平庸的僕人把主人給他的一千銀子埋在地裏。

27 Light

John Milton

Though hard and rare: thee I revisit safe,
And feel thy sovran vital Lamp; but thou
Revisit'st not these eyes, that rowle in vain
To find thy piercing ray, and find no dawn;
So thick a drop serene hath quencht thir Orbs,
Or dim suffusion veild. Yet not the more
Cease I to wander where the Muses haunt
Cleer Spring, or shadie Grove, or Sunnie Hill,
Smit with the love of sacred song; but chief
Thee *Sion* and the flowrie Brooks beneath
That wash thy hallowd feet, and warbling flow,
Nightly I visit: nor somtimes forget
Those other two equal'd with me in Fate,
So were I equal'd with them in renown.
Blind Thamyris and blind Mæonides,
And Tiresias and Phineus Prophets old.
Then feed on thoughts, that voluntarie move
Harmonious numbers; as the wakeful Bird

本詩為節譯本，原詩首二十行未錄。
(1)詩人原在描寫地獄，現在開始描寫人間，因而再向詩神（你）呼籲，請他幫助。
(2)這裏說的詩神，是聖詩之神攸雷尼亞（Urania）；

二十七 向光呼籲

約翰・彌爾頓

我又能安然訪問你(1)，
感受到你的常明燈火了；但是呵，
這兩眼却與你無緣：它們盡翻轉，
想窺見天日，却不見一線曙光；
是一層內障阻隔了眼睛的映像，
或翳蒙遮住了光線。但我不因此
便懶於徘徊在詩神漫遊的仙境：
我依然熱愛詩歌裏的清泉，
茂林，向陽的山坡；然而每夜裏
我主要尋訪的却是你(2)，郇山和山下
洗濯你的聖足的流水潺湲的
百花溪泉；我也不時地想起
那兩個和我遭同樣運命的詩人
（但願我也能跟他們同享聲譽），
失明的塞米里斯(3)和米歐尼迪斯(4)，
也想起古先知迪里夏斯，斐尼斯；
然後我凝神醞釀能激起和美
詩句的情思；像那不眠之鳥(5)，

　　他住在耶路撒冷的聖地。
(3)神話中的詩人。
(4)即荷馬。
(5)即夜鶯。

Sings darkling, and in shadiest Covert hid
Tunes her nocturnal Note. Thus with the Year
Seasons return, but not to me returns
Day, or the sweet approach of Ev'n or Morn,
Or sight of vernal bloom, or Summers Rose,
Or flocks, or herds, or human face divine;
But cloud in stead, and ever-during dark
Surrounds me, from the chearful waies of men
Cut off, and for the Book of knowledg fair
Presented with a Universal blanc
Of Natures works to mee expung'd and ras'd,
And wisdome at one entrance quite shut out.
So much the rather thou Celestial light
Shine inward, and the mind through all her powers
Irradiate, there plant eyes, all mist from thence
Purge and disperse, that I may see and tell
Of things invisible to mortal sight.

暗地裏歌唱，在林木深深的地方，
試奏着夜曲。於是，年年都有
四季輪轉，但是，我這裏却永遠
輪不到白晝，美好的晨光與暮色，
或是盛春的繁英，初夏的玫瑰，
或羊羣，牛羣，或人類神美的容顏；
恰恰相反，我的週圍是烏雲，
和永不散化的黑暗，人間的交往，
已跟我絕斷，知識的書本已闔起，
自然現象，好像在眼前塗抹掉，
茫然一片，恰如無字的紙篇，
智慧的一重門戶已被關嚴。
因此，神聖的光呵，只好請你
照耀我內心，使我的內心素質
璀璨發光；請你在這裏植慧眼，
從這裏驅散雲障；我這樣才能
瞧見並講出凡人瞧不見的景象。

殷寶書譯

28 Epigram on Milton

John Dryden

Three poets, in three distant ages born,
Greece, Italy, and England did adorn.
The first in loftiness of thought surpassed;
The next in majesty; in both the last.
The force of Nature could no farther go;
To make a third she joined the former two.

屈拉頓（1631—1700），生於英國諾坦普頓郡。詩歌題材多樣化，包括《獎章》（*The Medal*）、《世俗的宗教》（*Religio Laici*）等。創作了各類戲劇共二十七部，其中著名的有《西班牙人征服格蘭納達》（*The Conquest of Granada by the Spaniards*）、

二十八　題彌爾頓畫像

　　　　　　　　　　約翰·屈拉頓

三位著名的詩人，
降生在三個遙遠的時代。
各自為希臘、意大利和英格蘭，
增添了奪目的光彩。

第一位憑高雅取勝，
第二位以雄渾見長。
第三位非同凡響：
兼有兩者之強。

原來是萬能的造化
除此外無法可想：
為塑造第三位寵兒，
惟有揉合兩者而取其所長！

　　　　　　　　　　黃源深譯
　　　　　　　　　　孫　梁校

《為了愛情》（*All for Love*）等。
　《題彌爾頓畫像》一詩刊印在1688年雅各布·湯森版《失樂園》內彌爾頓畫像下，詩中提及的三位詩人是荷馬、維吉爾和彌爾頓。

29 Ode on Solitude

Alexander Pope

Happy the man whose wish and care
   A few paternal acres bound,
Content to breathe his native air,
        In his own ground.

Whose herds with milk, whose fields with bread,
   Whose flocks supply him with attire,
Whose trees in summer yield him shade,
        In winter fire.

Blest, who can unconcernedly find
   Hours, days, and years slide soft away,
In health of body, peace of mind,
        Quiet by day,

Sound sleep by night; study and ease,
   Together mixed; sweet recreation;
And innocence, which most does please
        With meditation.

蒲伯（1688—1744），生於倫敦。十六歲時寫成《田園詩》(*Pastorals*)，立即名噪一時。他的作品多用英雄偶句體（heroic couplet），著名作品有《卷髮遇劫記》(*The Rape of the Lock*)，英譯荷馬

二十九　隱居頌

亞歷山大・蒲伯

他是那樣歡樂欣喜，
只企求數公頃祖傳土地。
他心滿意足地呼吸故鄉的空氣，
——在他自己擁有的田園裏。

牲畜供他牛奶，土地賜他麵包，
羊羣呵給了他衣袍。
樹木在夏天送來蔭凉，
到冬日又使他不愁柴草。

他是如此幸福滿足，
超然地任光陰悄悄流淌。
心平氣和，體格健壯，
寧靜地度過白晝時光。

夜晚他睡得爛熟，
因爲他勞逸兼顧不忘閒游。
他那令人喜愛的單純質樸，
溶合在沉思默想的時候。

的《伊利亞特》(*Iliad*)和《奧德賽》(Odyssey)。
　　《隱居頌》一詩讚美了大自然和超脫塵世的獨居生活。

Thus let me live, unseen, unknown;
    Thus unlamented let me die;
Steal from the world, and not a stone
        Tell where I die.

我願活着無人見無人曉，
我願死時亦無人哀悼。
讓我從這世界悄悄溜走，
連頑石也不知我在何處躺倒。

黃源深譯
孫　梁校

30 Elegy Written in a Country Churchyard (Extract)

Thomas Gray

The curfew tolls the knell of parting day,
   The lowing herd wind slowly o'er the lea,
The plowman homeward plods his weary day,
   And leaves the world to darkness and to me.

Now fades the glimmering landscape on the sight,
   And all the air a solemn stillness holds,
Save where the beetle wheels his droning flight,
   And drowsy tinklings lull the distant folds:

...

The Epitah

Here rests his head upon the lap of Earth
   A youth to Fortune and to Fame unknown.
Fair Science frowned not on his humble birth,
   And Melancholy marked him for her own.

Large was his bounty, and his soul sincere,

    葛雷(1716−1771)，生於倫敦，後就學於劍橋。
1738年周遊歐洲大陸，三年後返英國劍橋定居。創作
極嚴謹，平生的詩作經他自己刪定者不足二十首。
    《鄉村墓地輓歌》一詩作於1750年，是葛雷最重

三十 鄉村墓地輓歌（節選）

托馬斯·葛雷

晚鐘殷殷響，夕陽已西沉。
羣牛呼叫歸，迂迴走草徑。
農夫荷鋤犁，倦倦回家門。
惟我立曠野，獨自對黃昏。

暮色何蒼茫，景物漸朦朧。
四野俱寂靜，無聲亦無風。
惟有小甲蟲，紛飛聲嗡嗡。
遠處玎玲響，羊羣進圈中。

……

墓誌銘

此地有青年，頭枕大地眠。
默默無名聲，坎坷又貧賤。
家境雖寒微，才華却超凡。
憂傷度青春，碌碌送華年。

施人旣慷慨，待人又忠誠。

要的作品。

　　全詩共三十二節，一百二十八行，現選錄首二節及末三節。

Heaven did a recompense as largely send:
He gave to Misery all he had, a tear,
He gained from Heaven ('twas all he wished) a friend.

No farther seek his merits to disclose,
Or draw his frailties from their dread abode,
(There they alike in trembling hope repose,)
The bosom of his Father and his God.

上天知憐才,深切寄同情。
在世不得志,眼中淚常盈。
天國有知己,神明知我心。

一生隨逝水,功名無可揚。
不需尋瑕疵,身在土中藏。
最後審判日,功過自昭彰。
身歸天父懷,靈魂入天堂。

豐華瞻譯

31 My Mary

William Cowper

The twentieth year is wellnigh past
Since first our sky was overcast;
Ah, would that this might be the last!
      My Mary!

Thy spirits have a fainter flow,
I see thee daily weaker grow;
'Twas my distress that brought thee low,
      My Mary!

Thy needles, once a shining store,
For my sake restless heretofore,
Now rust disused, and shine no more;
      My Mary!

For though thou gladly wouldst fulfil
The same kind office for me still,
Thy sight now seconds not thy will,
      My Mary!

柯珀（1731－1800），英國早期浪漫主義的先驅詩人，出身教士家庭。重要作品爲後期的《任務》(*The Task*)、《約翰・吉爾賓》(*John Gilpin*)等。1791年發表荷馬史詩的譯本。

三十一 我的瑪麗

威廉・柯珀

從咱們頭上烏雲初次陰翳，
二十個年頭即將消逝；
但願這是最後一次！
我的瑪麗啊！

你精神逐漸萎頓，
我看你日益消沉；
是我的痛苦使你萎靡不振，
我的瑪麗啊！

你用的針曾閃閃發光，
爲了我它們一直在忙。
如今生銹，不再閃耀光芒。
我的瑪麗啊！

雖然你還樂於爲我操勞，
替我縫補破衣襖，
你的目力已衰，力不從心了。
我的瑪麗啊！

　　柯珀長期寄住於恩溫（Unwin）家中，把不少詩篇獻給慈祥的女主人瑪麗・恩溫。《我的瑪麗》以素韵詩體（blank verse）寫成，是其中感人至深的一篇。

But well thou play'dst the housewife's part,
And all thy threads with magic art
Have wound themselves about this heart,
        My Mary!

Thy indistinct expressions seem
Like language utter'd in a dream;
Yet me they charm, whate'er the theme,
        My Mary!

Thy silver locks, once auburn bright,
Are still more lovely in my sight
Than golden beams of orient light,
        My Mary!

For could I view nor them nor thee,
What sight worth seeing could I see?
The sun would rise in vain for me,
        My Mary!

Partakers of thy sad decline,
Thy hands their little force resign;
Yet, gently press'd, press gently mine,
        My Mary!

Such feebleness of limbs thou prov'st,

你爲了家務日夜辛勤,
魔術般的巧手,一綫綫一針針,
都纏繞着我的心靈;
我的瑪麗啊!

你模糊的喃喃細語,
像睡眠中發出的夢囈;
不管你說的什麽話題,我都感到有趣;
我的瑪麗啊!

你銀白的秀髮曾閃耀栗色光澤;
如今在我眼中仍比東方旭日
金色的光芒更有魅力;
我的瑪麗啊!

假如我看不見你的頭髮,看不見你,
世上還有什麽值得我看的東西?!
太陽徒然昇起,我總是索然無味。
我的瑪麗啊!

你可悲地日益衰弱,
你那雙手也愈來愈軟弱,
然而,我輕輕握緊你手,你也輕輕握緊;
我的瑪麗啊!

你的四肢軟弱到極度,

That now at every step thou mov'st
Upheld by two; yet still thou lov'st,
      My Mary!

And still to love, though press'd with ill,
In wintry age to feel no chill,
With me is to be lovely still,
      My Mary!

But ah! by constant heed I know
How oft the sadness that I show
Transforms thy smiles to looks of woe,
      My Mary!

And should my future lot be cast
With much resemblance of the past,
Thy worn-out heart will break at last —
      My Mary!

而今每走一步都得靠兩人扶；
然而你的愛仍使我感觸，
我的瑪麗啊！

儘管你病體不支，你的慈愛始終不渝。
到了暮年並不覺得雪冷風淒；
在我眼中你仍秀美無比；
我的瑪麗啊！

唉！我經常注意而感到：
多少次我流露的苦惱
使你的笑容變得烏雲籠罩；
我的瑪麗啊！

假如我未來的命運，
還像過去那樣不幸，
你衰竭的心將破損——
我的瑪麗啊！

吳興祿譯
孫　梁校

32 Reeds of Innocence

William Blake

Piping down the valleys wild,
  Piping songs of pleasant glee,
On a cloud I saw a child,
  And he laughing said to me:

"Pipe a song about a Lamb!"
  So I piped with merry cheer.
"Piper, pipe that song again;"
  So I piped: he wept to hear.

"Drop thy pipe, thy happy pipe;
  Sing thy songs of happy cheer!"
So I sung the same again,
  While he wept with joy to hear.

"Piper, sit thee down and write
  In a book that all may read."
So he vanish'd from my sight;
  And I pluck'd a hollow reed,

三十二　天真之歌

威廉·布萊克

我吹着牧笛從荒谷下來，
我吹出歡樂的曲調，
我看見雲端上一個小孩，
他笑着對我說道：

"吹一支羔羊的歌曲！"
我就快活地吹了起來。
"吹笛人，再吹吹那支曲，"
我再吹，他聽着流下淚來。

"放下那笛子，歡樂的笛子，
把你那快樂的歌兒唱一唱；"
我把那支歌再唱一次，
他聽着，快活得淚兒汪汪。

"吹笛人，坐下來寫成一本詩，
好讓大伙兒都能讀到。"
他說完就從我眼前消逝，
我拿起一根空心的蘆草，

　　布萊克（1757－1827），英國詩人兼畫家，自幼學習版畫，此後一生靠刻版畫過活。1783年正式出版詩集《詩的素描》，後來的詩集多由詩人親手刻印，如《經驗之歌》（*Songs of Experience*）。

And I made a rural pen,
    And I stain'd the water clear,
And I wrote my happy songs
    Every child may joy to hear.

用它做成土氣的筆一枝，
把它蘸在清清的水裏，
寫下那些快樂的歌子，
讓個個小孩聽得歡喜。

　　　　　　　　袁可嘉譯

33 The Tiger

William Blake

Tiger, tiger, burning bright
In the forests of the night,
What immortal hand or eye
Could frame thy fearful symmetry?

In what distant deeps or skies
Burnt the fire of thine eyes?
On what wings dare he aspire?
What the hand dare seize the fire?

And what shoulder and what art
Could twist the sinews of thy heart?
And, when thy heart began to beat,
What dread hand and what dread feet?

What the hammer? What the chain?
In what furnace was thy brain?
What the anvil? What dread grasp
Dare its deadly terrors clasp?

When the stars threw down their spears,
And water'd heaven with their tears,
Did He smile His work to see?

三十三　老　虎

威廉・布萊克

老虎！老虎！你金色輝煌，
火似地照亮黑夜的林莽，
什麼樣超凡的手和眼睛
能塑造你這可怕的勻稱？

在什麼樣遙遠的海底天空，
燒出給你做眼睛的火種？
憑什麼樣翅膀他胆敢高翔？
敢於攫火的是什麼樣手掌？

什麼樣技巧，什麼樣肩頭，
能扭成你的心臟的肌肉？
等到你的心一開始跳躍，
什麼樣嚇壞人的手和脚？

什麼樣鐵鏈？什麼樣鐵鎚？
什麼樣熔爐煉你的腦髓？
什麼樣鐵砧？什麼樣握力
敢捏牢這些可怕的東西？

當星星射下來萬道金輝，
並在天空裏遍灑着珠淚，
看了看這傑作他可曾微笑？

Did He who made the lamb make thee?

Tiger, tiger, burning bright
In the forests of the night,
What immortal hand or eye
Dare frame thy fearful symmetry?

造小羊的可不也造了你了？

老虎！老虎！你金色輝煌，
火似地照亮黑夜的林莽，
什麼樣超凡的手和眼睛
敢塑造你這可怕的勻稱？

宋雪亭譯

34 The Chimney Sweeper

William Blake

A little black thing among the snow,
Crying "weep, weep" in notes of woe!
"Where are thy father and mother, say?" —
"They are both gone up to church to pray.

"Because I was happy upon the heath,
And smiled among the winter's snow,
They clothed me in the clothes of death,
And taught me to sing the notes of woe.

"And because I am happy, and dance and sing,
They think they have done me no injury,
And are gone to praise God and his Priest and King,
Who make up a heaven of our misery."

三十四　掃烟囱的小孩

威廉・布萊克

白雪裏有個小小的黑東西，
"掃烟！掃烟！"喊叫得慘凄！
"孩子！你爸爸媽媽在哪裏？"
"他倆都去教堂禱告上帝。

"只因我在家鄉跳來蹦去，
又在冬天雪地裏嬉笑，
他們便給我穿上這喪衣，
還教我唱這凄涼調。

"又因我唱歌跳舞挺歡暢，
他們認爲對我沒有傷害，
便去讚美上帝、牧師和君王，
用我們的痛苦來造一個樂園。"

吳興祿譯
孫　梁校

35 My Heart's in the Highlands

Robert Burns

(Chorus)
My heart's in the Highlands, my heart is not here;
My heart's in the Highlands, a-chasing the deer,
A-chasing the wild deer, and following the roe —
My heart's in the Highlands wherever I go.

Farewell to the Highlands, farewell to the North!
The birthplace of valour, the country of worth;
Wherever I wander, wherever I rove,
The hills of the Highlands for ever I love.

Farewell to the mountains high covered with snow!
Farewell to the straths and green valleys below!
Farewell to the forests and wild-hanging woods!
Farewell to the torrents and loud-pouring floods!

(Chorus)
My heart's in the Highlands, my heart is not here;
My heart's in the Highlands a-chasing the deer,

三十五　我的心呀在高原

羅伯特・彭斯

（合唱）
我的心呀在高原，這兒沒有我的心，
我的心呀在高原，追趕着鹿羣，
追趕着野鹿，跟蹤着小鹿，
我的心呀在高原，別處沒有我的心！

再會吧，高原！再會吧，北方！
你是品德的國家、壯士的故鄉！
不管我在哪兒遊蕩，到哪兒流浪，
高原的羣山我永不相忘！

再會吧，白雪皚皚的高山！
再會吧，綠色的山谷同河灘！
再會吧，高聳的大樹，無盡的林濤！
再會吧，洶湧的急流，雷鳴的浪潮！

（合唱）
我的心呀在高原，這兒沒有我的心，
我的心呀在高原，追趕着鹿羣，

彭斯（1759－1796），蘇格蘭詩人，生於窮困園丁之家，自十三歲起到三十多歲一直做農務工作。大部份作品用蘇格蘭本土方言寫成。

A-chasing the wild deer, and following the roe —
My heart's in the Highlands wherever I go!

追趕着野鹿,跟蹤着小鹿,
我的心呀在高原,別處沒有我的心!

王佐良譯

36 'A Man's a Man for A' That

Robert Burns

Is there, for honest poverty,
   That hangs his head, an' a' that,
The coward slave, we pass him by,
   We dare be poor for a' that!
     For a' that an' a' that,
       Our toil's obscure, an' a' that;
       The rank is but the guinea's stamp,
       The man's the gowd for a' that.

What tho' on hamely fare we dine,
   Wear hodden-grey, an' a' that;
Gie fools their silks, and knaves their wine,
   A man's a man for a' that.
     For a' that, an' a' that,
       Their tinsel show, an' a' that;
       The honest man, tho' e'er sae poor,
       Is king o' men for a' that.

Ye see yon birkie ca'd a lord
   Wha struts, an' stares, an' a' that;
Tho' hundreds worship at his word,
   He's but a coof for a' that
     For a' that, an' a' that,

三十六　不管那一套

羅伯特・彭斯

有沒有人,為了正大光明的貧窮
而垂頭喪氣,挺不起腰——
這種怯懦的奴才,我們不齒他!
我們敢於貧窮,不管他們那一套,
管他們這一套那一套,
什麼低賤的勞動那一套,
官銜只是金幣上的花紋,
人才是眞金,不管他們那一套!

我們吃粗糧,穿破爛,
但那又有什麼不好?
讓蠢才穿羅著緞,壞蛋飲酒作樂,
大丈夫是大丈夫,不管他們那一套!
管他們這一套那一套,
他們是繡花枕頭,
正大光明的人,儘管窮得要死,
才是人中之王,不管他們那一套!

你瞧那個叫做老爺的傢伙
裝模作樣,大擺大搖,
儘管他一呼百諾,
儘管他有勛章綬帶一大套,
白痴還是白痴!

    His ribband, star, an' a' that,
    The man o' independent mind,
    He looks an' laughs at a' that.

A prince can mak a belted knight,
 A marquis, duke, an' a' that;
But an honest man's aboon his might,
 Guid faith, he maunna fa' that!
   For a' that, an' a' that,
    Their dignities, an' a' that,
    The pith o' sense, an' pride o' worth,
    Are higher rank than a' that.

Then let us pray that come it may,
 As come it will for a' that,
That sense and worth, o'er a' the earth,
 Shall bear the gree, an' a' that.
   For a' that, an' a' that,
    It's coming yet, for a' that,
    That man to man, the world o'er,
    Shall brithers be for a' that.

管他們這一套那一套,
一個有獨立人格的人
看了只會哈哈大笑!

國王可以封官:
公侯伯子男一大套。
光明正大的人不受他管——
他也別夢想弄圈套!
管他們這一套那一套,
什麼貴人的威儀那一套,
實實在在的真理,頂天立地的品格,
才比什麼爵位都高!

好吧,讓我們來為明天祈禱,
不管怎麼變化,明天一定會來到,
那時候真理和品格
將成為整個地球的榮耀!
管他們這一套那一套,
總有一天會來到:
那時候全世界所有的人
都成了兄弟,不管他們那一套!

王佐良譯

37 Scots Wha Ha'e

Robert Burns

Scots, wha ha'e wi' Wallace bled,
Scots, wham Bruce has aften led;
Welcome to your gory bed,
    Or to victorie!
Now's the day, and now's the hour;
See the front o' battle lour;
See approach proud Edward's power —
    Chains and slaverie!

Wha will be a traitor knave?
Wha can fill a coward's grave?
Wha sae base as be a slave?
    Let him turn and flee!
Wha for Scotland's king and law
Freedom's sword will strongly draw,
Freeman stand or freeman fa',
    Let him follow me!

《蘇格蘭人》是彭斯愛國詩中最著名的一首，寫蘇格蘭國王羅伯特·布魯斯在大破英軍的班諾克本一役（1314年）前向部隊所作的號召。最先發表於1794

三十七　蘇格蘭人

羅伯特・彭斯

跟華萊士⑴流過血的蘇格蘭人，
隨布魯斯作過戰的蘇格蘭人，
起來！倒在血泊裏也成——
　　　　要不就奪取勝利！

時刻已到，決戰已近，
前綫的軍情吃緊，
驕橫的愛德華⑵在統兵入侵——
　　　　帶來鎖鏈，帶來奴役！

誰願賣國求榮？
誰願爬進懦夫的墳塋？
誰卑鄙到寧做奴隸偸生？——
　　　　讓他走，讓他逃避！

誰願將蘇格蘭國王和法律保護，
拔出自由之劍來痛擊、猛舞？
誰願生作自由人，死作自由魂？——
　　　　讓他來，跟我出擊！

年5月。
⑴十三世紀蘇格蘭民族英雄，曾大敗英軍。
⑵指英王愛德華二世。

By oppression's woes and pains!
By your sons in servile chains!
We will drain our dearest veins,
   But they shall be free!
Lay the proud usurpers low!
Tyrants fall in every foe!
Liberty's in every blow! —
   Let us do or die!

憑被壓迫者的苦難來起誓，
憑你們受奴役的子孫來起誓，
我們決心流血到死——
　　　　但他們必須自由！

打倒驕橫的篡位者！
死一個敵人，少一個暴君！
多一次攻擊，添一分自由！
　　　動手——要不就斷頭！

　　　　　　　　　　王佐良譯

38 A Red, Red Rose

Robert Burns

O my luve is like a red, red rose,
    That's newly sprung in June;
O my luve is like the melodie
    That's sweetly played in tune.

As fair thou art, my bonie lass,
    So deep in luve am I;
And I will luve thee still, my dear,
    Till a' the seas gang dry.

Till a' the seas gang dry, my dear,
    And the rocks melt wi' the sun;
And I will luve thee still, my dear,
    While the sands o' life shall run.

And fare thee weel, my only luve,
    And fare thee weel a while;
And I will come again, my luve,
    Tho' it were ten thousand mile!

三十八　一朵紅紅的玫瑰

羅伯特·彭斯

啊，我愛人像紅紅的玫瑰，
　　在六月裏苞放；
啊，我愛人像一支樂曲，
　　樂聲美妙、悠揚。

你那麼美，漂亮的姑娘，
　　我愛你那麼深切；
我會永遠愛你，親愛的，
　　一直到四海涸竭。

直到四海涸竭，親愛的，
　　直到太陽把岩石消鎔！
我會永遠愛你，親愛的，
　　只要生命無窮。

再見吧，我唯一的愛人，
　　再見吧，小別片刻！
我會回來的，我的愛人，
　　即使萬里相隔！

袁可嘉譯
孫　梁校

39 John Anderson, My Jo

Robert Burns

John Anderson my jo, John,
   When we were first acquent,
Your locks were like the raven,
   Your bonie brow was brent;
But now your brow is beld, John,
   Your locks are like the snow,
But blessings on your frosty pow,
   John Anderson, my jo!

John Anderson my jo, John,
   We clamb the hill thegither
And mony a canty day, John,
   We've had wi' ane anither:
Now we maun totter down, John,
   And hand in hand we'll go,
And sleep thegither at the foot,
   John Anderson, my jo!

三十九　約翰·安徒生，我愛

羅伯特·彭斯

約翰·安徒生，我愛，
　想咱倆當初相識，
你的臉容光潔，
　你的頭髮烏黑；
如今你毛髮脫掉，約翰，
　你的稀髮雪白；
約翰·安徒生，我愛！
　祝福你白頭尚健！

約翰·安徒生，我愛，
　咱倆曾一起登山；
多少個快活日子，約翰，
　咱倆曾一起歡暢；
如今得蹣跚下坡，約翰，
　咱倆一起走，手攙手；
約翰·安徒生，我愛！
　到山腳下長眠相守。

袁可嘉譯
孫　梁校

40 Lucy Gray

William Wordsworth

I travell'd among unknown men
  In lands beyond the sea;
Nor, England! did I know till then
  What love I bore to thee.

'Tis past, that melancholy dream!
  Nor will I quit thy shore
A second time; for still I seem
  To love thee more and more.

Among thy mountains did I feel
  The joy of my desire;
And she I cherish'd turn'd her wheel
  Beside an English fire.

Thy mornings show'd, thy nights conceal'd
  The bowers where Lucy play'd;
And thine too is the last green field
  That Lucy's eyes survey'd.

沃茲沃斯（1770—1850），出身律師家庭，與柯爾律奇、騷賽同被稱為"湖畔派"(the Lake School)詩人。1798年與柯爾律奇共同創作出版詩集《抒情謠曲》(*Lyrical Ballads*)。作品產量極豐，重要作

四十　露西抒情詩

威廉・沃茲沃斯

我曾在陌生人中間作客，
　　在那遙遠的海外；
英格蘭！那時，我才懂得
　　我對你多麼摯愛。

終於過去了，那淒涼的夢境！
　　我再不離開你遠游；
我心中對你的蜜意深情
　　時間愈久愈醇厚。

在你的山嶽中，我終於獲得
　　我衷心嚮往的安恬；
我心愛的人兒搖着紡車，
　　坐在英格蘭爐邊。

你晨光展現的，你夜幕遮掩的
　　是露西遊憩過的林園；
露西最後一眼望見的
　　是你那青碧的草原……

　　　　　　　　　　楊德豫譯

品有長詩《漫游》(*The Excursion*)等。
　《露西抒情詩》共五首，都與一位名叫露西的女子有關。

41 The Solitary Reaper

William Wordsworth

Behold her, single in the field,
Yon solitary Highland Lass!
Reaping and singing by herself;
Stop here, or gently pass!
Alone she cuts and binds the grain,
And sings a melancholy strain;
O listen! for the Vale profound
Is overflowing with the sound.

No Nightingale did ever chaunt
More welcome notes to weary bands
Of travellers in some shady haunt,
Among Arabian sands;
A voice so thrilling ne'er was heard
In spring-time from the Cuckoo-bird,
Breaking the silence of the seas
Among the farthest Hebrides.

Will no one tell me what she sings? —
Perhaps the plaintive numbers flow

四十一　孤獨的割禾女

威廉・沃茲沃斯

你瞧那孤獨的山地少女，
　一個人在田裏，割着，唱着；
別驚動她呵，快停下脚步，
　　要不就輕輕走過！
她獨自收割，獨自捆好，
唱的是一支幽怨的曲調；
你聽！這一片清越的音波
已把那深深的山谷淹沒。

夜鶯哪有這樣美的歌吟
　來安慰那些困乏的旅客——
當他們找到了棲宿的樹蔭，
　　在那阿拉伯大漠？
杜鵑的歌喉怎及她宛轉——
當它們在春日縱情啼囀，
在千里迢迢的赫布里底(1)，
啼聲劃破了海上的岑寂？

誰能告訴我她唱些什麼？
　也許這淒婉的歌聲是詠嘆

---

(1)赫布里底羣島，在蘇格蘭以西，由五百多個大小島
　嶼組成。

131

For old, unhappy, far-off things,
And battles long ago;
Or is it some more humble lay,
Familiar matter of today?
Some natural sorrow, loss, or pain,
That has been, and may be again?

Whate'er the theme, the Maiden sang
As if her song could have no ending;
I saw her singing at her work,
And o'er the sickle bending; —
I listen'd, motionless and still;
And, as I mounted up the hill,
The music in my heart I bore,
Long after it was heard no more.

古老的、遙遠的悲歡離合，
　　往昔年代的征戰？
要麼是一支平凡的曲子，
唱的是當今的尋常瑣事？
常見的痛苦，失意，憂傷，
歷來是如此，今後也一樣？

這姑娘，不論唱的是什麼，
　　彷彿能唱個沒完沒了；
只見她一邊唱、一邊幹活，
　　彎腰揮動着鐮刀；——
我一動不動，悄悄聽着；
直到我緩步登上山坡，
那歌調早已寂無聲響，
却還在心底悠悠回蕩。

楊德豫譯

42 The Daffodils

William Wordsworth

I wander'd lonely as a cloud
   That floats on high o'er vales and hills,
When all at once I saw a crowd,
   A host, of golden daffodils;
Beside the lake, beneath the trees,
Fluttering and dancing in the breeze.

Continuous as the stars that shine
   And twinkle on the Milky Way,
They stretch'd in never-ending line
   Along the margin of a bay:
Ten thousand saw I at a glance,
Tossing their heads in sprightly dance.

The waves beside them danced, but they
   Out-did the sparkling waves in glee:
A poet could not but be gay
   In such a jocund company!
I gazed — and gazed — but little thought
What wealth the show to me had brought:

For oft, when on my couch I lie
   In vacant or in pensive mood,

四十二　水仙

威廉・沃兹沃斯

獨自漫游似浮雲，
　　青山翠谷上飄荡；
一剎那瞥見一叢叢、
　　一簇簇水仙金黃；
樹蔭下，明湖邊，
　　和風吹拂舞翩躚。

彷彿羣星璀璨，
　　沿銀河閃爍晶瑩；
一灣碧波邊緣，
　　綿延，望不盡；
只見萬千無窮，
隨風偃仰舞興濃。

花邊波光瀲灔，
　　怎比得繁花似錦；
面對如此艮伴，
　　詩人怎不歡欣！
凝視，凝視，流連不止；
殊不知引起悠悠情思：

兀自倚榻憩息，
　　岑寂，幽然冥想；

135

They flash upon that inward eye
    Which is the bliss of solitude;
And then my heart with pleasure fills,
And dances with the daffodils.

驀地花影閃心扉，
　獨處方能神往；
衷心喜悅洋溢，
伴水仙，舞不息。

孫梁譯

43 Upon Westminster Bridge

William Wordsworth

Earth has not anything to show more fair:
    Dull would he be of soul who could pass by
    A sight so touching in its majesty:
This City now doth, like a garment, wear

The beauty of the morning; silent, bare,
    Ships, towers, domes, theatres, and temples lie
    Open unto the fields, and to the sky,
All bright and glittering in the smokeless air.

Never did sun more beautifully steep
    In his first splendour valley, rock, or hill;
Ne'er saw I, never felt, a calm so deep!

    The river glideth at his own sweet will:
Dear God! the very houses seem asleep;
    And all that mighty heart is lying still!

四十三　威斯敏斯特橋上有感

威廉·沃兹沃斯

大地無處呈現更壯麗的景象：
　氣象萬千，如此沁人心脾；
　倘若漠視，必然心靈麻痺。
此刻都市宛如披上晨裝：

冠帶華嚴，沉寂而曠遠；
　船、塔、穹頂、劇場和寺院
　躺延至原野、天邊，
在清澈的朝氣中閃現。

晨曦映射金光萬道，
　普照幽谷、巉岩、山崗；
如斯靜謐從未感到！

　河水潺潺流，悠然自得；
上帝呵！萬家華屋似酣睡，
　宏大的心臟[1]悄然安息。

孫梁譯

———————

[1]指倫敦。

44 To the Cuckoo

William Wordsworth

O blithe new-comer! I have heard,
I hear thee and rejoice.
O Cuckoo! shall I call thee Bird,
Or but a wandering Voice?

While I am lying on the grass
Thy twofold shout I hear;
From hill to hill it seems to pass
At once far off, and near.

Though babbling only to the Vale,
Of sunshine and of flowers,
Thou bringest unto me a tale
Of visionary hours.

Thrice welcome, darling of the Spring!
Even yet thou art to me
No bird, but an invisible thing,
A voice, a mystery;

The same whom in my schoolboy days
I listened to; that Cry
Which made me look a thousand ways

四十四　致布穀鳥

威廉・沃茲沃斯

啊，快樂的新客！
　　聽到你囀鳴，我滿懷喜悅；
啊，布穀，是否稱你鳥？
　　或為妙音，迴盪清越？

當我躺在草地上，
　　聽到你的雙重唱：
似從這山傳到那山，
　　似在近旁，又在遠方。

你的歌聲在山谷迴盪，
　　伴着繁花和陽光；
你還把我帶到
　　追憶往事的幻想。

我再三地歡迎
　　你是陽春的先行。
在我眼中，你可不是鳥，
　　而是無形的神奇之音。

想當年我還是小學生，
　　曾傾聽同樣的鳴聲；
我千方百計尋找，

In bush, and tree, and sky.

To seek thee did I often rove
Through woods and on the green;
And thou wert still a hope, a love;
Still longed for, never seen.

And I can listen to thee yet;
Can lie upon the plain
And listen, till I do beget
That golden time again.

O blessèd Bird! the earth we pace
Again appears to be
An unsubstantial, faery place;
That is fit home for Thee!

從天上找到叢林。

我時常漫遊，為了找你，
　　踩着草地，穿過密林；
如今仍在期待，雖不眼見，
　　你仍是希望，是戀情。

此刻我躺在平原，
　　你的歌聲仍能聽見。
我專心諦聽，
　　直到召回金色的童年。

我們棲息的大地
　　又顯得空靈而神奇；
這是你安家的福地，
　　啊，快樂的鳥兒，祝福你！

　　　　　　　　　　　吳興祿譯
　　　　　　　　　　　孫　梁校

45 Hunting Song

Walter Scott

Waken, lords and ladies gay,
On the mountain dawns the day;
All the jolly chase is here
With hawk and horse and hunting-spear;
Hounds are in their couples yelling,
Hawks are whistling, horns are knelling,
Merrily merrily mingle they,
"Waken, lords and ladies gay."

Waken, lords and ladies gay,
The mist has left the mountain gray,
Springlets in the dawn are steaming,
Diamonds on the brake are gleaming;
And foresters have busy been
To track the buck in thicket green;
Now we come to chant our lay
"Waken, lords and ladies gay."

Waken, lords and ladies gay,

司各特(1771-1832)，生於蘇格蘭，曾當律師、出版商和地方長官。重要作品有長篇敘事詩《瑪米恩》(*Marmion*)、《湖上貴婦》(*Lady of the Lake*)等，反映蘇格蘭的史跡。1814年後轉向創作歷史小

四十五　行獵歌

華爾德・司各特

醒來吧，快樂的老爺太太們，
山間已是清晨；
飛鷹走馬，揮槍舞矛，
追呀趕呀好不熱鬧；
號角鳴，兀鷹嘯，
獵犬成對狂號，
繁音交響，一片歡聲——
"醒來吧，快樂的老爺太太們！"

醒來吧，快樂的老爺太太們，
山間晨霧已散盡；
涓涓細流，水汽騰騰，
漫漫綠野，露珠瑩瑩；
一頭公鹿，藏身樹叢，
守林人忙着追蹤；
讓我們唱一曲，正是良辰——
"醒來吧，快樂的老爺太太們！"

醒來吧，快樂的老爺太太們，

說。

　　《行獵歌》採用了叠句的形式，富有民謠風味，是司各特作品的特色。

To the greenwood haste away;
We can show you where he lies,
Fleet of foot and tall of size;
We can show the marks he made
When 'gainst the oak his antlers fray'd;
You shall see him brought to bay;
"Waken, lords and ladies gay."

Louder, louder chant the lay
Waken, lords and ladies gay!
Tell them youth and mirth and glee
Run a course as well as we;
Time, stern huntsman! who can baulk,
Stanch as hound and fleet as hawk;
Think of this, and rise with day,
Gentle lords and ladies gay!

快到綠林來,別磨蹭;
那公鹿身高腿又快,
我們會給您指明白:
哪棵橡樹下它匍伏安身,
樹幹上有鹿角的擦痕;
你們必將看它陷入絕境——
"醒來吧,快樂的老爺太太們!"

唱吧,唱吧,高聲再高聲,
醒來吧,快樂的老爺太太們!
告訴他們:歡樂和青春
稍縱即逝,猶如人生;
時光似獵手,嚴峻逼人!
無情如獵狗,迅疾如兀鷹;
思量吧,何不早起身,
高貴而快樂的老爺太太們!

陸壽筠譯
孫　梁校

46　The Pride of Youth

Walter Scott

Proud Maisie is in the wood,
    Walking so early;
Sweet Robin sits on the bush,
    Singing so rarely.

"Tell me, thou bonny bird,
    When shall I marry me?"
— "When six braw gentlemen
    Kirkward shall carry ye."

"Who makes the bridal bed,
    Birdie, say truly?"
— "The gray-headed sexton
    That delves the grave duly.

"The glowworm o'er grave and stone
    Shall light thee steady;
The owl from the steeple sing,
    Welcome, proud lady."

四十六　青春的驕傲

華爾德・司各特

驕傲的梅西漫步林間，
　　踩着晨曦；
伶俐的知更鳥棲息樹叢，
　　唱得甜蜜。

"告訴我，美麗的鳥兒，
　　我哪年哪月穿嫁裝？"——
"等到六個殯葬人
　　抬你上教堂。"

"誰爲我鋪新床？
　　好鳥兒，莫撒謊。"——
"白髮司事，兼挖墓穴，
　　誤不了你的洞房。

"螢火蟲幽幽閃閃，
　　把你的墳墓照亮，送葬，
貓頭鷹將在塔尖高唱：
　　歡迎你，驕傲的姑娘。"

陸壽筠譯

孫　梁校

47 The Rime of the Ancient Mariner (Extract)

Samuel Taylor Coleridge

PART 1

It is an ancient Mariner,
And he stoppeth one of three.
"By thy long grey beard and glittering eye,
Now wherefore stopp'st thou me?

The Bridegroom's doors are opened wide,
And I am next of kin;
The guests are met, the feast is set:
May'st hear the merry din."

He holds him with his skinny hand,
"There was a ship," quoth he.
"Hold off! unhand me, grey-beard loon!"
Eftsoons his hand dropt he.

He holds him with his glittering eye —
The Wedding-Guest stood still,
And listens like a three years' child:
The Mariner hath his will.

The Wedding-Guest sat on a stone:

柯爾律奇(1772—1834),英國詩人及文學評論家;1796年出版第一本詩集,其後翻譯了德國席勒(*Schiller*)的詩劇《華倫斯坦之死》(*Wallenstein's Tod*)。主要作品有《克麗斯特貝爾》(*Christabel*)、《忽必烈汗》(*Kubla Khan*)等,並有文藝評論作品《文學評傳》(*Bio-*

四十七 老舟子行（節選）

賽繆爾・泰勒・柯爾律奇

第 一 章

那是一個老年舟子，
　　三人中攔住一人。
"目光炯炯的這老漢，
　　你攔我為甚原因？

新郎家前大門洞啓，
　　我最親被召婚筵。
賓客到齊，排了酒席——
　　聽那邊笑語喧闐。"

他用如柴手掌抓住：
　　"我當初在一舟中——"
"站開！放手，羊鬚老漢！"
　　他聞言立刻手鬆。

但他雙眼有如磁鐵，

---

graphia Literaria)。

《老舟子行》分七章，每行基本為八音節 (*octo-syllabic*)，着意刻劃老水手的形象，並加插各種奇特的情節。現選錄首末二章。

He cannot choose but hear;
And thus spake on that ancient man,
The bright-eyed Mariner.

"The ship was cheered, the harbour cleared,
Merrily did we drop
Below the kirk, below the hill,
Below the lighthouse top.

The Sun came up upon the left,
Out of the sea came he!
And he shone bright, and on the right
Went down into the sea.

Higher and higher every day,
Till over the mast at noon —"
The Wedding-Guest here beat his breast,
For he heard the loud bassoon.

The bride hath paced into the hall,
Red as a rose is she;
Nodding their heads before her goes
The merry minstrelsy.

The Wedding-Guest he beat his breast,
Yet he cannot choose but hear;

令喜賓不得不留
在路旁，靠石頭坐下，
　　聽老人數說根由。

"船拔錨碇離開泊岸，
　　行駛過莊嚴教堂，
旋出羅盤似的山影，
　　越燈塔，到水中央。

日頭在水左方升上，
　　過蒼蒼似是孤帆。
他待長庚出來時候
　　向右方擲下金丸。

一天過去高似一天，
　　直到交午桅竿上——"
喜賓急得雙手搥胸，
　　因他聞笛聲嘹喨：

新婦已經步到堂上，
　　臉緋紅好像薔薇。
在她前面，鼓腮點首，
　　樂師將簫管高吹。

喜賓急得搥胸搓掌，
　　但他仍不得不留

And thus spake on that ancient man,
The bright-eyed Mariner.

"And now the STORM-BLAST came, and he
Was tyrannous and strong:
He struck with his o'ertaking wings,
And chased us south along.

With sloping masts and dipping prow,
As who pursued with yell and blow
Still treads the shadow of his foe,
And forward bends his head,
The ship drove fast, loud roared the blast,
And southward aye we fled.

And now there came both mist and snow,
And it grew wondrous cold:
And ice, mast-high, came floating by,
As green as emerald.

And through the drifts the snowy clifts
Did send a dismal sheen:
Nor shapes of men nor beasts we ken —
The ice was all between.

The ice was here, the ice was there,
The ice was all around:
It cracked and growled, and roared and howled,

在路旁，靠石頭坐下，
　　聽老人續述根由。

"忽然暴風捲起洋面，
　　萬里中但見洪波，
我們的船向南刮去，
　　舟中人徒喚奈何。

檣傾斜着，首沒水中，
　　如巨人低頭追敵：
我們的船，破浪乘風，
　　向南奔一時不息。

我們駛入霧同白雪，
　　地峭寒不可留停，
桅竿高的冰山漂過，
　　翡翠般碧綠晶瑩。

浮冰之外尙多雪嶺，
　　射過來慘淡光輝，
不見人影，亦無獸跡，
　　只堅冰環繞周圍。

航過一程還是冰島，
　　更航行晶嶺當前：
牠們畢剝，喧豗，澎湃，

155

Like noises in a swound!

At length did cross an Albatross,
Thorough the fog it came;
As if it had been a Christian soul,
We hailed it in God's name.

It ate the food it ne'er had eat,
And round and round it flew.
The ice did split with a thunder-fit;
The helmsman steered us through!

And a good south wind sprung up behind;
The Albatross did follow,
And every day, for food or play,
Came to the mariner's hollo!

In mist or cloud, or mast or shroud,
It perched for vespers nine;
Whiles all the night, through fog-smoke white,
Glimmered the white Moon-shine."

"God save thee, ancient Mariner!
From the fiends, that plague thee thus! —
Why look'st thou so?" — With my cross-blow
I shot the ALBATROSS.

如暈時聲震耳邊。

有一海鴨穿過濃霧，
　牠向船冉冉飛來。
我們見牠似逢故友，
　拍手呼，樂滿胸懷。

我們取食充牠饑腹，
　牠在空反復翱翔。
冰山忽爆，舵工取道
　載我們逃出中央！

起了南風，吹舟北上，
　後方那海鴨緊跟。
每天取食，或是玩耍。
　牠聞呼即便來臨。

霧裏，雲中，檣頭，帆上，
　牠總共停了九天。
這九天內，穿過濃霧，
　有月光亮在夜間。"

"你的雙目何以發光，
　如魔鬼附身，舟子？
天保佑你！""是我彎弓
　一箭將海鴨射死！"

PART 7

This Hermit good lives in that wood
Which slopes down to the sea.
How loudly his sweet voice he rears!
He loves to talk with marineres
That come from a far countree.

He kneels at morn, and noon, and eve —
He hath a cushion plump:
It is the moss that wholly hides
The rotted old oak-stump.

The skiff-boat neared: I heard them talk,
"Why, this is strange, I trow!
Where are those lights so many and fair,
That signal made but now?"

"Strange, by my faith!" the Hermit said —
"And they answered not our cheer!
The planks looked warped! and see those sails,
How thin they are and sere!
I never saw aught like to them,
Unless perchance it were

Brown skeletons of leaves that lag
My forest-brook along;
When the ivy-tod is heavy with snow,

……

第七章

他獨居在海邊林內。
　晨與昏高唱頌詩。
他喜問訊遠游舟子
　在船歸故國之時。

他有膝墊柔如絨製,
　祈禱時日用三回:
那是橡樹餘的根節,
　苔生滿上面,周圍。

小舟近時我聞言語,
　"這樁事真正稀奇:
剛才看見紅光相召,
　走來了那知被欺!"

隱士也道,"奇怪,奇怪。
　我們喚不聽回聲——
船板裂了!那些帆布
　薄如紙又顯凋零:

似黃葉懸樹的骨架,
　在藤蘿覆雪時光,

And the owlet whoops to the wolf below,
That eats the she-wolf's young."

"Dear Lord! it hath a fiendish look —
(The Pilot made reply)
I am a-feared" — "Push on, push on!"
Said the Hermit cheerily.

The boat came closer to the ship,
But I nor spake nor stirred;
The boat came close beneath the ship,
And straight a sound was heard.

Under the water it rumbled on,
Still louder and more dread:
It reached the ship, it split the bay;
The ship went down like lead.

Stunned by that loud and dreadful sound,
Which sky and ocean smote,
Like one that hath been seven days drowned
My body lay afloat;
But swift as dreams, myself I found
Within the Pilot's boat.

Upon the whirl, where sank the ship,
The boat spun round and round;
And all was still, save that the hill

上頭有梟怪聲叫喚,
　　狼在下吞食小狼。"

"這船看來形狀不妙,
　　我不敢還向前划,"
領港人說。"划上前去,"
　　隱士拏慰語相加。

小舟向我慢慢行近,
　　我無言亦未挪身。
小舟到了我的船下,
　　港水中忽發大聲:

隆隆有似雷霆下降,
　　愈近時聲響愈高。
觸上船時一聲爆裂,
　　船如鉛立沈怒濤。

這聲炸裂驚天動海,
　　震得我魂飛耳聾——
等我悠悠魂魄清醒,
　　見己身在小舟中。

那條船在漩渦之內
　　螺絲樣沈入波瀾。
波紋漸大漸漸消滅,

Was telling of the sound.

I moved my lips — the Pilot shrieked
And fell down in a fit;
The holy Hermit raised his eyes,
And prayed where he did sit.

I took the oars: the Pilot's boy,
Who now doth crazy go,
Laughed loud and long, and all the while
His eyes went to an fro.
"Ha! ha!" quoth he, "full plain I see,
The Devil knows how to row."

And now, all in my own countree,
I stood on the firm land!
The Hermit stepped forth from the boat,
And scarcely he could stand.

"O shrieve me, shrieve me, holy man!"
The Hermit crossed his brow.
"Say quick," quoth he, "I bid thee say —
What manner of man art thou?"

Forthwith this frame of mine was wrenched
Wtih a woful agony,
Which forced me to begin my tale;
And then it left me free.

剩四圍迴響空山。

領港人才見我開口，
　一聲叫便倒船頭。
隱士也將雙目高舉，
　唇動着向天默求。

瘋了領港人的兒子。
　他見我盪槳清波，
"我知道了，哈哈！"他笑，
　"鬼也會划船渡河。"

我這已經脚登實地？
　我已經回了家鄉？
隱士也從舟中上岸。
　他軟如醉漢郎當。

"救我，救我！"我求隱士。
　他舉手合十胸襟，
"你說，你說，"他開言道，
　"你是鬼還是生人？"

我聞此語抽了一下，
　如利刀割我心肝。
不得不將往事詳叙。
　叙畢時方覺泰然。

Since then, at an uncertain hour,
That agony returns:
And till my ghastly tale is told,
This heart within me burns.

I pass, like night, from land to land;
I have strange power of speech;
That moment that his face I see,
I know the man that must hear me:
To him my tale I teach.

What loud uproar bursts from that door!
The wedding-guests are there:
But in the garden-bower the bride
And bride-maids singing are:
And hark the little vesper bell,
Which biddeth me to prayer!

'O Wedding-Guest! this soul hath been
Alone on a wide wide sea:
So lonely 'twas, that God himself
Scarce scemèd there to be.

O sweeter than the marriage-feast,
'Tis sweeter far to me,
To walk together to the kirk
With a goodly company! —

To walk together to the kirk
And all together pray,
While each to his great Father bends,
Old men, and babes, and loving friends
And youths and maidens gay!

此後常來一陣劇痛
　　　　盤踞在我的心頭，
　　必要前事重述一遍，
　　　　心靈內方覺自由。

　　從此我的談鋒健利。
　　　　我如夜飄過四方。
　　何人應聽我的故事，
　　　　我一眼便知端詳。

　　你聽那邊來的喧鬧！
　　　　是堂上賓客熙雍。
　　新婦料必歌唱園內。
　　　　但我喜晚聞禱鐘——

　　因我當時漂流大海，
　　　　四周圍不見生人，
　　望中只有連天波浪，
　　　　船板上便是屍身！——

　　熱鬧場中非我所喜，
　　　　我只喜偕同信徒
　　在神座前懺悔罪孽，
　　　　讓鐘聲淨滌前汙。

Farewell, farewell! but this I tell
To thee, thou Wedding-Guest!
He prayeth well, who loveth well
Both man and bird and beast.

He prayeth best, who loveth best
All things both great and small;
For the dear God who loveth us,
He made and loveth all.

The Mariner, whose eye is bright,
Whose beard with age is hoar,
Is gone: and now the Wedding-Guest
Turned from the bridegroom's door.

He went like one that hath been stunned,
And is of sense forlorn:
A sadder and a wiser man,
He rose the morrow morn.

赴宴之賓，別了，別了！
　但聽我臨別囑言：
"愛你同類並及禽獸，
　祈禱時神始垂憐。

能愛萬物，無論小大，
　祈禱時神耳始傾。
因爲上天造成萬物，
　無大小皆他寧馨。"

目光炯炯的那舟子，
　年壽高鬢已斑斑，
他去了。喜賓如有失，
　轉身行，躲避聲喧。

他似臨頭澆了冷水，
　興頭已無影無蹤。
他從此便識透悲樂，
　將舟子常憶心中。

　　　　　　　　　朱湘譯

48 Finis

Walter Savage Landor

I strove with none, for none was worth my strife.
Nature I loved and, next to Nature, Art:
I warm'd both hands before the fire of life;
It sinks, and I am ready to depart.

蘭德(1775—1864),生於英國瓦立克郡(*Warwick*),1798 年出版第一本詩集,其中代表作是《蓋比爾》(*Gebir*); 1847 年出版最後一本詩集《擬希臘詩》(*The Hellenics*)。散文創作有《幻想談話錄》五册

四十八　終　曲

沃爾特・薩凡基・蘭德

與世無爭兮性本狷介。
鍾情自然兮游心藝苑；
生命之火兮暖我心田，
爝火熄兮羽化而歸天。

孫梁譯

(*Imaginary Conversations*)。
　　《終曲》是蘭德最受人傳誦的作品，對仗工整自然，意味雋永。

49 There Was a Sound of Revelry by Night

George Gordon Byron

There was a sound of revelry by night,
And Belgium's capital had gathered then
Her Beauty and her Chivalry, and bright
The lamps shone o'er fair women and brave men,
A thousand hearts beat happily; and when
Music arose with its voluptuous swell,
Soft eyes looked love to eyes which spake again,
And all went merry as a marriage bell;
But hush! hark! a deep sound strikes like a rising knell!

Did ye not hear it? — No; 'twas but the wind,
Or the car rattling o'er the stony street;
On with the dance! let joy be unconfined;
No sleep till morn, when Youth and Pleasure meet
To chase the glowing hours with flying feet —
But hark! — that heavy sound breaks in once more,
As if the clouds its echo would repeat;
And nearer, clearer, deadlier than before!

拜倫(1788—1824),生於倫敦,十歲時繼承爵位。1816年妻子要求分居,詩人備受上層人士譭謗攻擊,移居意大利。1823年投入希臘爭取獨立之戰,翌年患黑熱症而死。重要作品有《恰爾德·哈洛德漫遊記》(*Childe Harold's Pilgrimage*)、《唐璜》(*Don Juan*)、《審判的幻景》(*The Vision of Judgment*)。

四十九　滑鐵盧前夜

喬治・戈登・拜倫

夜深深，縱飲狂歡，樂不可支，
比利時京城從四處集聚了一廳
那麼些美貌再加那麼些英姿，
華燈把美女英雄照得好鮮明；
千顆心快樂的跳着；然後只一聽
蕩人心魄的音樂海潮樣四湧，
溫柔的眼睛跟眼睛就反覆傳情，
大家都歡欣鼓舞得像結婚打鐘；
可是聽！聽啊！什麼聲音像喪鐘的轟隆！

你們聽見嗎？——沒有；無非是颶風，
或者是車輪在石街上滾得太笨；
繼續跳舞吧！讓大家樂一個無窮；
青春逢喜悅，睡覺且等到早晨，
飛鞋急步一齊趕煥發的良辰——
可是聽！——那種沉重的聲音又來鬧，
雲端像把它的回聲又重複一陣；
近了，更近了，越來越可怕，越高！

　　《滑鐵盧前夜》選自《恰爾德・哈洛德漫遊記》第三卷，題目為譯者所加。滑鐵盧位於比利時首都近郊，1815年英軍在此駐扎。呂希蒙公爵夫人設宴款待英軍將士，拿破崙乘其不備，於當晚突然襲擊。本詩腳韻排列是ababbcbcc。

Arm! Arm! it is — it is — the cannon's opening roar!

Ah! then and there was hurrying to and fro,
And gathering tears, and tremblings of distress,
And cheeks all pale, which but an hour ago
Blushed at the praise of their own loveliness;
And there were sudden partings, such as press
The life from out young hearts, and choking sighs
Which ne'er might be repeated; who could guess
If ever more should meet those mutual eyes,
Since upon night so sweet such awful morn could rise!

And there was mounting in hot haste: the steed,
The mustering squadron, and the clattering car,
Went pouring forward with impetuous speed,
And swiftly forming in the ranks of war;
And the deep thunder peal on peal afar;
And near, the beat of the alarming drum
Roused up the soldier ere the morning star;
While thronged the citizens with terror dumb,
Or whispering, with white lips — "The foe! they come! they come!"

抗槍！抗槍！這是——這是——人家開大砲！

啊！立刻到處是紛紛亂亂，
涕淚縱橫，難過到直抖，直顫動，
臉龐都發白，全不像一小時以前
一聽到讚美它們就那樣羞紅；
到處是突兀的離別，年輕的心胸
壓走了生命，嗚咽得說不成話，
多分再無從說了；誰又猜得中
是否還能見那些眼睛的應答，
旣然是夜這樣可愛，早晨就這樣可怕！

到處是急急匆匆的上馬：戰馬，
集合的騎隊，砲車震響個不停，
紛紛都火急飛快的向戰地出發，
頃刻間一排排都列成作戰的隊形；
遠處是一陣又一陣深沉的雷鳴；
近處是報警的銅鼓一齊打開了，
不等到啓明星就催起所有的士兵；
老百姓擠在一起，都給嚇呆了，
或者戰兢兢悄悄說——"敵人來了，來了！"

卞之琳譯

50 When We Two Parted

George Gordon Byron

When we two parted
 In silence and tears,
Half broken-hearted
 To sever for years,
Pale grew thy cheek and cold,
 Colder thy kiss;
Truly that hour foretold
 Sorrow to this!

The dew of the morning
 Sunk chill on my brow —
It felt like the warning
 Of what I feel now.
Thy vows are all broken,
 And light is thy fame:
I hear thy name spoken,
 And share in its shame.

They name thee before me,
 A knell to mine ear;
A shudder comes o'er me —
 Why wert thou so dear?
They know not I knew thee

五十　昔日依依別

喬治·戈登·拜倫

昔日依依別,
淚流默無言;
離恨肝腸斷,
此別又幾年。
冷頰何慘然,
一吻寒更添;
日後傷心事,
此刻已預言。

朝起寒露重,
凜冽凝眉間——
彼時已預告:
悲傷在今天。
山盟今安在?
汝名何輕賤!
吾聞汝名傳,
羞愧在人前。

聞汝名聲惡,
猶如聽喪鐘。
不禁心怵惕——
往昔情太濃。
誰知舊日情,

    Who knew thee too well:
Long, long shall I rue thee,
    Too deeply to tell.

In secret we met —
    In silence I grieve,
That thy heart could forget,
    Thy spirit deceive.
If I should meet thee
    After long years,
How should I greet thee?
    With silence and tears.

斯人知太深。
綿綿長懷恨,
盡在不言中,

昔日喜幽會,
今朝恨無聲。
舊情汝已忘,
痴心遇薄倖。
多年離別後,
抑或再相逢,
相逢何所語?
淚流默無聲。

陳錫麟譯

孫　梁校

51 Childe Harold's Pilgrimage

Canto I: XIII (Interlude)

George Gordon Byron

Adieu, adieu! my native shore
Fades o'er the waters blue;
The Night-winds sigh, the breakers roar,
And shrieks the wild sea-mew.
Yon Sun that sets upon the sea
We follow in his flight;
Farewell awhile to him and thee,
My native Land — Good Night!

A few short hours and He will rise
To give the morrow birth;
And I shall hail the main and skies,
But not my mother earth.
Deserted is my own good hall,
Its hearth is desolate;
Wild weeds are gathering on the wall;
My dog howls at the gate.

"Come hither, hither, my little page!

五十一　《恰爾德·哈洛德漫遊記》
第一卷第十三節（插曲）

喬治·戈登·拜倫

永別，永別了！祖國海岸
消逝在碧藍水涯；
晚風嗚咽，波濤澎湃，
海鷗淒厲地尖嘯。
游子悵望斜陽，
天邊紅日落海面；
再見了，夕陽，還有您，
我的故鄉——再見！

不久旭日又會映紅
另一個清晨；
我將歡呼海闊天空，
但故國沉淪。
家園荒蕪人烟稀，
爐火呵熄滅；
野藤攀緣頹壁，
愛犬門邊吠。

"來吧，來吧，我的書童(1)，

《恰爾德·哈洛德漫遊記》於1812年問世，是拜倫在1809年遍遊歐洲後的作品。
(1)以下是公子哈洛德（拜倫的化身）與書童的對話。

Why dost thou weep and wail?
Or dost thou dread the billows' rage,
Or tremble at the gale?
But dash the tear-drop from thine eye;
Our ship is swift and strong:
Our fleetest falcon scarce can fly
More merrily along."

"Let winds be shrill, let waves roll high,
I fear not wave nor wind;
Yet marvel not, Sir Childe, that I
Am sorrowful in mind;
For I have from my father gone,
A mother whom I love,
And have no friend, save these alone,
But thee — and one above.

"My father bless'd me fervently,
Yet did not much complain;
But sorely will my mother sigh
Till I come back again."
"Enough, enough, my little lad!
Such tears become thine eye;
If I thy guileless bosom had,

為何悲悲戚戚？
你怕怒濤洶湧？
風暴使你顫慄？
擦掉淚水別擔心，
這船堅固迅捷，
超過疾飛的兀鷹，
乘風破浪如箭。"

"任憑風嘯浪滔天(1)，
不怕浪，不怕風；
但我心中悲哀，
主人請聽下情：
我跟您飄泊海上，
遠離父母膝前，
沒有朋友交往，
惟有您——和蒼天。

老父為我熱烈祝福，
並不怎麼抱怨；
可慈母將傷心長嘆，
直到兒回家園。"
"別哭，別哭，小兒郎！
淚水使人心疼；
假如我天眞，像你一樣，

---

(1)以下為書童答話。

Mine own would not be dry."

"Come hither, hither, my staunch yeoman,
Why dost thou look so pale?
Or dost thou dread a French foeman?
Or shiver at the gale?"
"Deem'st thou I tremble for my life?
Sir Childe, I'm not so weak;
But thinking on an absent wife
Will blanch a faithful cheek.

"My spouse and boys dwell near thy hall,
Along the bordering lake,
And when they on their father call,
What answer shall she make?"
"Enough, enough, my yeoman good,
Thy grief let none gainsay;
But I, who am of lighter mood,
Will laugh to flee away.

"For who would trust the seeming sighs
Of wife or paramour?
Fresh fares will dry the bright blue eyes
We late saw streaming o'er."

也會淚珠晶瑩。"

"來吧,來吧,堅貞的僕人⑴,
為何臉色蒼白?
你怕同法國人交鋒?
或被狂風嚇破膽?"
"您以為我嚇得要命?
主人,我並不膽怯;
可惦記離別的女人,
忠實的丈夫怎不悲切?!

我妻兒在您莊園附近,
宅邊湖畔住下;
要是兒子喊父親,
媽媽怎麼回答?!"
"別擔憂,別擔憂,好僕人,
你的悲傷是真心;
但我比你看得輕,
一笑置之不操心。

妻子情婦都裝腔,
假惺惺,誰相信?!——
藍色明眸,淚注雙頰;
見新歡,笑盈盈!"

⑴以下是哈洛德與另一僕人的對話。

For pleasures past I do not grieve,
Nor perils gathering near;
My greatest grief is that I leave
No thing that claims a tear.

And now I'm in the world alone,
Upon the wide, wide sea:
But why should I for others groan,
When none will sigh for me?
Perchance my dog will whine in vain,
Till fed by stranger hands;
But long ere I come back again
He'd tear me where he stands.

With thee, my bark, I'll swiftly go
Athwart the foaming brine;
Nor care what land thou bear'st me to,
So not again to mine.
Welcome, welcome, ye dark-blue waves!
And when you fail my sight,
Welcome, ye deserts, and ye caves!
My native Land — Good Night!

昔日歡樂如烟雲，
災難臨頭不驚；
最可悲莫如心冷，
不需人憐憫！

想如今我孑然一身，
飄零在浩瀚的海上；
我何必爲別人呻吟，
既然無人爲我悲傷。
或許愛犬徒然哀鳴，
直到陌生人來喂養；
但多年後我回家門，
它將狂吠，猙獰惡相。

扁舟呵，我將和你流浪，
伴隨迸濺的海沫；
任你把游子載向何方，
反正無計歸宿。
歡迎，歡迎，紫藍色海波！
你們消逝了……
歡迎呵，沙漠！歡迎呵，岩窟！
我的故鄉——永別了！

孫　梁譯

52 The Isles of Greece

George Gordon Byron

The isles of Greece! the isles of Greece
   Where burning Sappho loved and sung,
Where grew the arts of war and peace,
   Where Delos rose, and Phoebus sprung!
Eternal summer gilds them yet,
But all, except their sun, is set.

The Scian and the Teian muse,
   The hero's harp, the lover's lute,
Have found the fame your shores refuse:
   Their place of birth alone is mute
To sounds which echo further west
Than your sires' "Islands of the Blest".

The mountains look on Marathon —

　　本詩為長篇敘事詩《唐·璜》(*Don Juan*)第三章中片段。
(1)莎孚（公元前 610—？），古希臘著名的抒情女詩人，作品大都是戀歌。
(2)蒂洛斯是愛琴海上島嶼，菲勃思即阿波羅(Phoebus Apollo)，希臘神話中司音樂詩歌與太陽之神。傳說蒂洛斯島從海底湧出，菲勃思降生島上。
(3)希臘在歐洲南方，經常陽光普照，氣候溫暖。
(4)Scian 由名詞 Scio 派生。Scio 即古代 Chios（凱

五十二 希臘羣島

喬治·戈登·拜倫

希臘羣島,希臘羣島!
　　火熱的莎孚(1)在此苦戀抒唱,
戰爭與和平的技能在此發揚;
　　蒂洛斯在此湧現,菲勃思茁長!(2)
永恒的夏日(3)仍使羣島閃金光,
但除了太陽,一切都已淪亡。

凱奧斯與泰奧斯兩尊詩神——
　　英雄的豎琴,情人的琵琶(4),
可惜在故鄉湮沒無聞——
　　對他們的名聲裝聾作啞;
但琴聲遠揚,傳遍西方,
超越你們祖宗的天堂。

羣山崔嵬,向着馬拉松(5)——

奧斯),愛琴海上大島,相傳爲詩人荷馬誕生地,故曰"凱奧斯詩神"。荷馬史詩主要詠述英雄業蹟,故曰"英雄的豎琴"。Teian由名詞Teos(泰奧斯)派生,小亞細亞海濱的古希臘城市,相傳是抒情詩人阿納克里恩(Anacreon)的故鄉,故曰"泰奧斯詩神"。阿納克里恩常於詩中讚美青春與愛情、醇酒和美女,故曰"情人的琵琶"。
(5)馬拉松,在雅典東北。公元前490年,波斯人大舉入侵希臘,在馬拉松被雅典軍擊潰。

And Marathon looks on the sea;
And musing there an hour alone,
   I dream'd that Greece might still be free;
For standing on the Persians' grave,
I could not deem myself a slave.

A king sate on the rocky brow
   Which looks o'er sea-born Salamis;
And ships, by thousands, lay below,
   And men in nations; — all were his!
He counted them at break of day —
And when the sun set, where were they?

And where are they? and where art thou,
   My country? On thy voiceless shore
The heroic lay is tuneless now —
   The heroic bosom beats no more!
And must thy lyre, so long divine,
Degenerate into hands like mine?

'Tis something in the dearth of fame,

馬拉松曠野，向着海洋；
在廢墟獨自冥思出神，
　夢想希臘尙能自由富强；
因爲屹立在波斯人墳上，
不能想像自己有奴隸相。

一位國王曾端坐懸崖上⑴，
　巉岩俯瞰海島薩拉密斯；
成千艨艟、百萬雄師在脚下，
　全歸他統率，頤指氣使！
他在淸晨檢閱，趾高氣揚，
但夕陽西下時，全被掃蕩！

艦隊在哪方？！還有您——祖國⑵，
　您在哪裏？在您無聲的岸邊
英勇的歌聲如今沉默——
　英勇的心臟停止跳躍！
您神聖的古琴如此悠久，
難道會墮入我這雙俗手？！

困在被奴役的民族中，

⑴國王指波斯王塞克西斯（Xerxes，公元前519？－465）。公元前480年，他統率波斯艦隊入侵希臘，在雅典附近的薩拉密斯島山崖上指揮觀戰。
⑵祖國表面上指希臘，深一層看，則指詩人的祖國。

Though link'd among a fetter'd race,
To feel at least a patriot's shame,
   Even as I sing, suffuse my face;
For what is left the poet here?
For Greeks a blush — for Greece a tear.

Must *we* but weep o'er days more blest?
   Must *we* but blush? — Our fathers bled.
Earth! render back from out thy breast
   A remnant of our Spartan dead!
Of the three hundred grant but three,
To make a new Thermopylae!

What, silent still? and silent all?
   Ah! no; — the voices of the dead
Sound like a distant torrent's fall,
   And answer, "Let one living head,
But one arise, — we come, we come!"
'Tis but the living who are dumb.

In vain — in vain: strike other chords;
   Fill high the cup with Samian wine!

雖無名聲，却有價值：
至少在歌唱時臉紅，
　感到愛國志士的耻辱；
詩人在此地有何留戀？
爲希臘人羞，爲希臘流淚。

難道我們只能悲泣懷古？
　我們只能羞慚？祖先却流血。
大地呵！從你懷抱裏交出
　幾個犧牲的斯巴達壯士！
三百人中只需三名，
讓塞摩辟烈⑴重顯威靈！

怎麼，仍然沉默？一切昏沉？
　呵！不——死者的回音
彷彿遠方激流喧騰，
　答道："只要一個活人，
一個挺身——我們就來，就來！"
可是活人麻木，都不理睬。

徒然，徒然；還是把調子換：
　斟滿大杯莎摩斯酒！⑵

───────

⑴塞摩辟烈，希臘東部險峻的關隘。公元前 480 年，
　波斯大軍入侵，斯巴達王李昂尼達斯（Leonidas）
　率領三百勇士抵擋，結果全體犧牲。
⑵莎摩斯是希臘羣島中較大的島，以釀製葡萄酒馳名。

Leave battles to the Turkish hordes,
    And shed the blood of Scio's vine!
Hark! rising to the ignoble call —
How answers each bold Bacchanal!

You have the Pyrrhic dance as yet;
    Where is the Pyrrhic phalanx gone?
Of two such lessons, why forget
    The nobler and the manlier one?
You have the letters Cadmus gave —
Think ye he meant them for a slave?

Fill high the bowl with Samian wine!
    We will not think of themes like these!
It made Anacreon's song divine:
    He served — but served Polycrates —
A tyrant; but our masters then
Were still, at least, our countrymen.

The tyrant of the Chersonese

---

(1)原文 Bacchanal 的詞源是 Bacchus，希臘神話中酒神，故 bacchanal 引伸為酒徒。

(2)原文 Pyrrhic 源自 Pyrrhus，古希臘城邦埃比勒斯（Epirus）的君主，作戰時擺密集的方陣著名。比利克舞蹈即模仿這種戰鬥方式。

(3)古希臘傳說人物，相傳他把腓尼基（Phoenicia,地中海邊古國）字母傳入希臘。

让土耳其蛮人去作战,
　　咱们来痛饮红葡萄酒!
听呀!可耻的召唤一发出,
酒鬼们⑴都欢呼,口水淌出!

你们仍然有比利克舞蹈,
　　可哪儿去找比利克方阵⑵?
两种宝贵遗产——为何忘掉
　　更崇高、更威武的一种?
卡德默思⑶为你们创造文字,
难道他是为奴隶费尽心思?!

斟满大杯莎摩斯酒!
　　咱们不想懊恼的事情!
还是想美妙神奇的歌手
　　阿纳克里恩⑷,他却侍奉暴君——
包里克雷狄⑸;但那时的主人
　　至少是希腊种,同根生。

克逊尼斯的霸王⑹,

⑷阿纳克里恩在波斯侵略时,逃往莎摩斯,依靠包里克雷狄庇护。

⑸包里克雷狄是莎摩斯岛君主,与波斯颉颃,颇有威名;这里称他 tyrant 含有原义"霸主"。

⑹克逊尼斯,在达达尼尔海峡之北,即现代的加列波里半岛。霸王指密尔达帝,曾统治该岛。波斯军大举入侵时,他任希腊联军统帅。

Was freedom's best and bravest friend;
That tyrant was Miltiades!
   O that the present hour would lend
Another despot of the kind!
Such chains as his were sure to bind.

Fill high the bowl with Samian wine!
   On Suli's rock, and Parga's shore,
Exists the remnant of a line
   Such as the Doric mothers bore;
And there, perhaps, some seed is sown,
The Heracleidan blood might own.

Trust not for freedom to the Franks —
   They have a king who buys and sells;
In native swords and native ranks
   The only hope of courage dwells:
But Turkish force and Latin fraud
Would break your shield, however broad.

Fill high the bowl with Samian wine!

---

(1)蘇里,希臘與阿爾巴尼亞之間山區;巴加,山區的港市。當時該區山民正與土耳其侵略軍英勇鬥爭,故詩人稱他們為古希臘英雄的子孫。

(2)原文Doric由Dorian(多利安人)派生。多利安人是古希臘最早的種族之一,後建斯巴達(Sparta)城。

捍衛民族自由,英勇非凡;
他是密爾達帝,千古流芳!
　呵!但願今天也出現
另一位霸主,同樣英明!
他那鐵腕定能團結軍民。

斟滿大杯莎摩斯酒!
　在蘇里山崗,巴加岸上⑴,
如今英勇的子孫尚存,
　宛如斯巴達母親哺養⑵;
那裏或許播下英雄艮種,
繼承赫古里斯的血統⑶。

爭自由不能靠西歐人⑷,
　他們的王收買又出賣;
只能靠本國的刀槍、士兵,
　才有希望勇敢作戰;
土耳其武力、西歐⑸的詐騙
會把你們巨大的盾牌砸扁。

斟滿大杯莎摩斯酒吧!
─────────

⑶Heracleidan 由 Heraclidae (海拉克里地人)派
　生。相傳海拉克里地人是希臘神話中大力神赫古里
　斯 (Hercules) 的後裔。此處指尚武的斯巴達人。
⑷原文 Franks 是地中海東部人民對西歐人的泛稱。
⑸Latin 並非僅指拉丁族人,而是泛指西歐各國。

  Our virgins dance beneath the shade —
I see their glorious black eyes shine;
  But gazing on each glowing maid,
My own the burning tear-drop laves,
To think such breasts must suckle slaves.

Place me on Sunium's marbled steep,
  Where nothing, save the waves and I,
May hear our mutual murmurs sweep;
  There, swan-like, let me sing and die:
A land of slaves shall ne'er be mine —
Dash down yon cup of Samian wine!

處女們在樹蔭下舞蹈——
黑幽幽眸子流盼閃霎；
　我凝視每個姑娘窈窕，
但美女乳汁將哺育奴隸，
令人熱淚盈眶而嘆息！

讓我登上蘇尼姆峭壁[1]，
　孑然一身，惟有山麓波浪
諦聽彼此絮語，傾訴衷曲；
　我願似天鵝，哀歌而死亡[2]，
決不苟延在奴隸的國土——
擲碎玉杯吧，美酒如糞土！

孫梁譯

---

[1]蘇尼姆，在雅典東南方雅典加（Attica）半島極南端，懸崖上有雅典的護城神雅典娜（Athena）廟宇。
[2]西方傳說，天鵝垂死時輒哀鳴。

53　Ode to the West Wind

Percy Bysshe Shelley

1

O wild West Wind, thou breath of Autumn's being
Thou, from whose unseen presence the leaves dead
Are driven, like ghosts from an enchanter fleeing,

Yellow, and black, and pale, and hectic red,
Pestilence-stricken multitudes: O thou,
Who chariotest to their dark wintry bed

The winged seeds, where they lie cold and low,
Each like a corpse within its grave, until
Thine azure sister of the Spring shall blow

Her clarion o'er the dreaming earth, and fill
(Driving sweet buds like flocks to feed in air)
With living hues and odors plain and hill:

Wild Spirit, which art moving everywhere;
Destroyer and preserver; hear, oh, hear!

雪萊（1792—1822），生於英國薩塞克斯郡。1816
年往瑞士，與拜倫結爲好友。1822年與友人駕帆船出
海，遇暴風，舟沉身亡。作品包括長詩《仙后麥布》

五十三　西風頌

波西・比希・雪萊

1

呵，狂野的西風，你把秋氣猛吹，
不露臉便將落葉一掃而空，
猶如法師趕走了羣鬼，

趕走那黃綠紅黑紫的一羣，
那些染上了瘟疫的魔怪——
呵，你讓種子長翅騰空，

又落在冰冷的土壤裏深埋，
像屍體躺在墳墓，但一朝
你那青色的東風妹妹回來，

為沉睡的大地吹響銀號，
驅使羊羣般的蓓蕾把大氣猛喝，
就吹出遍野嫩色，處處香飄。

狂野的精靈！你吹遍了大地山河，
破壞者，保護者，聽吧——聽我的歌！

(*Queen Mab*)、《阿多尼斯》(*Adonais*)等。

　　《西風頌》，全詩五節，每節的韻腳安排是：aba, bcb, cdc, ded, ee。

2

Thou on whose stream, 'mid the steep sky's commotion,
Loose clouds like earth's decaying leaves are shed,
Shook from the tangled boughs of Heaven and Ocean,

Angels of rain and lightning: there are spread
On the blue surface of thine airy surge,
Like the bright hair uplifted from the head

Of some fierce Maenad, even from the dim verge
Of the horizon to the zenith's height,
The locks of the approaching storm. Thou dirge

Of the dying year, to which this closing night
Will be the dome of a vast sepulchre,
Vaulted with all thy congregated might

Of vapours, from whose solid atmosphere
Black rain, and fire, and hail will burst: oh, hear!

3

Thou who didst waken from his summer dreams
The blue Mediterranean, where he lay,
Lulled by the coil of his crystalline streams,

2

你激荡長空，亂雲飛墜
如落葉；你搖撼天和海，
不許它們像老樹纏在一堆；

你把雨和電趕了下來，
只見藍空上你騁馳之處
忽有萬丈金髮披開，

像是酒神的女祭司勃然大怒，
愣把她的長髮遮住了半個天，
將暴風雨的來臨宣佈。

你唱着輓歌送別殘年，
今夜這天空宛如圓形的大墓，
罩住了混濁的雲霧一片，

却擋不住電火和冰雹的突破，
更有黑雨傾盆而下！呵，聽我的歌！

3

你驚擾了地中海的夏日夢，
它在清澈的碧水裏靜躺，
聽着波浪的催眠曲，睡意正濃，

Beside a pumice isle in Baiae's bay,
And saw in sleep old palaces and towers
Quivering within the wave's intenser day,

All overgrown with azure moss and flowers
So sweet, the sense faints picturing them! Thou
For whose path the Atlantic's level powers

Cleave themselves into chasms, while far below
The sea-blooms and the oozy woods which wear
The sapless foliage of the ocean, know

Thy voice, and suddenly grow gray with fear,
And tremble and despoil themselves: oh, hear!

4

If I were a dead leaf thou mightest bear;
If I were a swift cloud to fly with thee;
A wave to pant beneath thy power, and share

The impulse of thy strength, only less free
Than thou, O uncontrollable! If even
I were as in my boyhood, and could be

The comrade of thy wanderings over Heaven,

朦朧裏它看見南國港外石島旁，
烈日下古老的宮殿和樓台
把影子投在海水裏晃蕩，

它們的牆上長滿花朵和蘚苔，
那香氣光想想也叫人醉倒！
你的來臨叫大西洋也驚駭，

它忙把海水劈成兩半，為你開道，
海底下有瓊枝玉樹安臥，
儘管深潛萬丈，一聽你的怒號

就聞聲而變色，只見一個個
戰慄，畏縮——呵，聽我的歌！

4

如果我能是一片落葉隨你飄騰，
如果我能是一朵流雲伴你飛行，
或是一個浪頭在你的威力下翻滾，

如果我能有你的銳勢和衝勁，
即使比不上你那不羈的奔放，
但只要能拾回我當年的童心，

我就能陪着你遨遊天上，

As then, when to outstrip thy skiey speed
Scarce seem'd a vision; I would ne'er have striven

As thus with thee in prayer in my sore need.
Oh, lift me as a wave, a leaf, a cloud!
I fall upon the thorns of life! I bleed!

A heavy weight of hours has chained and bowed
One too like thee: tameless, and swift, and proud.

5

Make me thy lyre, even as the forest is:
What if my leaves are falling like its own!
The tumult of thy mighty harmonies

Will take from both a deep, autumnal tone,
Sweet though in sadness. Be thou, Spirit fierce,
My spirit! Be thou me, impetuous one!

Drive my dead thoughts over the universe
Like withered leaves to quicken a new birth!
And, by the incantation of this verse,

Scatter, as from an unextinguished hearth
Ashes and sparks, my words among mankind!

那時候追上你未必是夢囈,
又何至淪落到這等頹喪,

祈求你來救我之急!
呵,捲走我吧,像捲落葉,波浪,流雲!
我跌在人生的刺樹上,我血流遍體!

歲月沉重如鐵鏈,壓着的靈魂
原本同你一樣:高傲,飄逸,不馴。

5

讓我做你的豎琴吧,就同森林一般,
縱然我們都葉落紛紛,又有何妨!
我們身上的秋色斑爛,

好給你那狂飈曲添上深沉的回響,
甜美而帶蒼凉。給我你迅猛的勁頭!
豪邁的精靈,化成我吧,借你的鋒芒,

把我的腐朽思想掃出宇宙,
掃走了枯葉好把新生來激發;
憑着我這詩韻做符咒,

猶如從未滅的爐頭吹出火花,
把我的話散佈在人羣之中!

Be through my lips to unawakened earth

The trumpet of a prophecy! O Wind,
If Winter comes, can Spring be far behind?

對那沉睡的大地，拿我的嘴當喇叭，

吹響一個預言！呵，西風，
如果冬天已到，難道春天還用久等？

王佐良譯

54 Ozymandias

Percy Bysshe Shelley

I met a traveller from an antique land
Who said: Two vast and trunkless legs of stone
Stand in the desert . . . Near them, on the sand,
Half sunk, a shattered visage lies, whose frown,
And wrinkled lip, and sneer of cold command,
Tell that its sculptor well those passions read
Which yet survive, stamped on these lifeless things,
The hand that mocked them and the heart that fed;
And on the pedestal these words appear:
"My name is Ozymandias, king of kings:
Look on my works, ye Mighty, and despair!"
Nothing beside remains. Round the decay
Of that colossal wreck, boundless and bare,
The lone and level sands stretch far away.

五十四 奥西曼提斯

波西·比希·雪莱

客自海外歸,曾見沙漠古國
有石像半毀,唯餘巨腿
蹲立沙礫間。像頭旁落,
半遭沙埋,但人面依然可畏,
那冷笑,那發號施令的高傲,
足見雕匠看透了主人的心,
才把那石頭刻得神情唯肖,
而刻像的手和像主的心
早成灰燼。像座上大字在目:
"吾乃萬王之王是也,
蓋世功業,敢叫天公折服!"
此外無一物,但見廢墟周圍,
　　　寂寞平沙空莽莽,
　　　伸向荒涼的四方。

王佐良譯

奧西曼提斯即公元前十三世紀的埃及王雷米西斯二世。他的墳墓在底比斯,形如一龐大的獅身人首像。

55 To —

Percy Bysshe Shelley

One word is too often profaned
    For me to profane it,
One feeling too falsely disdain'd
    For thee to disdain it;
One hope is too like despair
    For prudence to smother,
And pity from thee more dear
    Than that from another.

I can give not what men call love:
    But wilt thou accept not
The worship the heart lifts above
    And the heavens reject not,
The desire of the moth for the star,
    Of the night for the morrow,
The devotion to something afar
    From the sphere of our sorrow?

五十五 致——

波西·比希·雪萊

有一個被人經常褻瀆的字,
　　我無心再來褻瀆;
有一種被人假意鄙薄的感情,
　　你不會也來鄙薄。
有一種希望太似絕望,
　　又何須再加提防!
你的憐憫無人能比,
　　溫暖了我的心房。

我拿不出人們所稱的愛情,
　　但不知你肯否接受
這顆心兒能獻的崇敬?
　　連天公也不會拒而不收!
猶如飛蛾撲向星星,
　　又如黑夜追求黎明,
這一種思慕遠處之情,
　　早已跳出了人間的苦境!

王佐良譯

56 Rise Like Lions

Percy Bysshe Shelley

Rise like Lions after slumber
In unvanquishable number —
Shake your chains to earth like dew
Which in sleep had fallen on you —
Ye are many — they are few.

本詩是長詩《暴政的假面具》(*The Mask of Anarchy*) 最後一節 (第91節)。1819年 8 月,英國曼徹斯特市工人羣起示威遊行,當局用騎兵鎮壓,工

五十六　像醒獅般奮起

波西・比希・雪萊

像醒獅般奮起反抗，
億萬成羣不可擋！
睡夢中鎖鏈套上身——
摔掉它，化爲灰燼；
他們一小撮，你們千萬人！

孫梁譯

人死傷甚多。雪萊義憤塡膺而寫此詩，故副標題是"爲曼徹斯特大屠殺所作"。

57 Music, When Soft Voices Die

Percy Bysshe Shelley

Music, when soft voices die,
Vibrates in the memory —
Odours, when sweet violets sicken,
Live within the sense they quicken.

Rose leaves, when the rose is dead,
Are heaped for the belovèd's bed;
And so thy thoughts, when thou art gone,
Love itself shall slumber on.

五十七 輕柔的聲音寂滅後

波西・比希・雪萊

輕柔的聲音寂滅後,
音樂將在回憶中蕩漾;
甘美的紫羅蘭枯萎後,
敏感的嗅覺中繚繞花香。

嬌艷的薔薇凋謝後,
花瓣將撒遍愛人的床;
同樣地,你消逝後,
思念將長眠於眷戀之鄉。

孫梁譯

58 Ode to a Nightingale

John Keats

My heart aches, and a drowsy numbness pains
   My sense, as though of hemlock I had drunk,
Or emptied some dull opiate to the drains
   One minute past, and Lethe-wards had sunk:
'Tis not through envy of thy happy lot,
     But being too happy in thine happiness —
        That thou, light-wingèd Dryad of the trees,
           In some melodious plot
   Of beechen green, and shadows numberless,
     Singest of summer in full throated ease.

O, for a draught of vintage! that hath been
   Cool'd a long age in the deep-delved earth,
Tasting of Flora and the country green,
   Dance, and Provençal song, and sunburnt mirth!
O for a beaker full of the warm South,
   Full of the true, the blushful Hippocrene,
      With beaded bubbles winking at the brim,
         And purple-stained mouth;

濟慈（1795—1821），曾習醫，但因熱愛文學而放棄行醫。1817年得雪萊的幫助，出版第一本詩集。1820年，肺病惡化，赴意大利養病，終病逝羅馬。作品包括《安狄米恩》（*Endymion*）、《聖亞尼節的前

五十八　夜鶯頌

約翰・濟慈

我的心在痛,困盹和麻木
　　刺進了感官,有如飲過毒鴆,
又像是剛剛把鴉片吞服,
　　於是向着列斯⑴忘川下沉:
並不是我嫉妒你的好運,
　　而是你的快樂使我太歡欣——
　　　　因爲在林間嘹喨的天地裏,
　　　　　　你呵,輕翅的仙靈,
　　你躱進山毛櫸的蔥綠和蔭影,
　　　　放開了歌喉,歌唱着夏季。

唉,要是有一口酒!那冷藏
　　在地下多年的清醇飲料,
一嘗就令人想起綠色之邦,
　　想起花神,戀歌,陽光和舞蹈!
要是有一杯南國的溫暖
　　充滿了鮮紅的靈感之泉,
　　　　杯沿明滅着珍珠的泡沫,
　　　　　　給嘴唇染上紫斑;

夕》(*The Eve of St. Agnes*)、《拉米亞》(*Lamia*)等。
⑴列斯,冥府中的河,鬼魂飲了它便忘記前生的一切,
　亦譯"忘川"。

That I might drink, and leave the world unseen,
      And with thee fade away into the forest dim:

Fade far away, dissolve, and quite forget
   What thou among the leaves hast never known,
The weariness, the fever, and the fret
   Here, where men sit and hear each other groan;
Where palsy shakes a few sad, last gray hairs,
   Where youth grows pale, and spectre-thin, and dies;
      Where but to think is to be full of sorrow
         And leaden-eyed despairs,
   Where Beauty cannot keep her lustrous eyes,
      Or new Love pine at them beyond to-morrow.

Away! away! for I will fly to thee,
   Not charioted by Bacchus and his pards,
But on the viewless wings of Poesy,
   Though the dull brain perplexes and retards:
Already with thee! tender is the night,
   And haply the Queen-Moon is on her throne,
      Cluster'd around by all her starry Fays;
         But here there is no light,
   Save what from heaven is with the breezes blown
      Through verdurous glooms and winding mossy ways.

I cannot see what flowers are at my feet,

哦，我要一飲而悄然離開塵寰，
　　和你同去幽暗的林中隱沒：

遠遠地、遠遠隱沒，讓我忘掉
　　你在樹葉間從不知道的一切，
忘記這疲勞、熱病、和焦躁，
　　這使人對坐而悲嘆的世界；
在這裏，青春蒼白、削瘦、死亡，
　　而"癱瘓"有幾根白髮在搖擺；
　　　在這裏，稍一思索就充滿了
　　　　憂傷和灰眼的絕望，
而"美"保持不住明眸的光彩，
　　新生的愛情活不到明天就枯凋。

去吧！去吧！我要朝你飛去，
　　不用和酒神坐文豹的車駕，
我要展開詩歌底無形羽翼，
　　儘管這頭腦已經困頓、疲乏；
去了！呵，我已經和你同往！
　　夜這般溫柔，月后正登上寶座，
　　　周圍是侍衞她的一羣星星；
　　　　但這兒却不甚明亮，
除了有一線天光，被微風帶過
　　葱綠的幽暗，和苔蘚的曲徑。

我看不出是哪種花草在脚旁，

Nor what soft incense hangs upon the boughs,
But, in embalmed darkness, guess each sweet
   Wherewith the seasonable month endows
The grass, the thicket, and the fruit-tree wild;
   White hawthorn, and the pastoral eglantine;
      Fast-fading violets cover'd up in leaves;
         And mid-May's eldest child,
   The coming musk-rose, full of dewy wine,
      The murmurous haunt of flies on summer eves.

Darkling I listen; and, for many a time
   I have been half in love with easeful Death,
Call'd him soft names in many a mused rhyme,
   To take into the air my quiet breath;
Now more than ever seems it rich to die,
   To cease upon the midnight with no pain,
      While thou art pouring forth thy soul abroad
         In such an ecstasy!
   Still wouldst thou sing, and I have ears in vain —
      To thy high requiem become a sod.

Thou wast not born for death, immortal Bird!
   No hungry generations tread thee down;
The voice I hear this passing night was heard
   In ancient days by emperor and clown:
Perhaps the self-same song that found a path

什麼清香的花掛在樹枝上；
在溫馨的幽暗裏，我只能猜想
　這個時令該把哪種芬芳
賦予這果樹，林莽，和草叢，
　這白枳花，和田野的玫瑰，
　　這綠葉堆中易謝的紫羅蘭，
　　　還有五月中旬的驕寵，
　這綴滿了露酒的麝香薔薇，
　　它成了夏夜蚊蚋的嗡營的港灣。

我在黑暗裏傾聽；呵，多少次
　我幾乎愛上了靜謐的死亡，
我在詩思裏用盡了好的言辭，
　求他把我的一息散入空茫；
而現在，哦，死更是多麼富麗：
　在午夜裏溘然魂離人間，
　　當你正傾瀉着你的心懷
　　　發出這般的狂喜！
　你仍將歌唱，但我却不再聽見——
　　你的葬歌只能唱給泥草一塊。

永生的鳥呵，你不會死去！
　飢餓的世代無法將你踩躪；
今夜，我偶然聽到的歌曲
　曾使古代的帝王和村夫喜悅；
或許這同樣的歌也曾激蕩

221

Through the sad heart of Ruth, when, sick for home,
    She stood in tears amid the alien corn;
        The same that oft-times hath
Charm'd magic casements, opening on the foam
    Of perilous seas, in faery lands forlorn.

Forlorn! the very word is like a bell
    To toll me back from thee to my sole self!
Adieu! the fancy cannot cheat so well
    As she is famed to do, deceiving elf.
Adieu! adieu! thy plaintive anthem fades
    Past the near meadows, over the still stream,
        Up the hill-side; and now 'tis buried deep
        In the next valley-glades:
Was it a vision, or a waking dream?
    Fled is that music: — Do I wake or sleep?

---

(1)據《舊約》，露絲是大衞王的祖先，原籍莫艾伯，以後在伯利恆爲富人波茲種田，並且嫁給了他。

(2)中世紀的傳奇故事往往描寫一個奇異的古堡，孤立在大海中；勇敢的騎士如果能冒險來到這裏，定會

露絲⑴憂鬱的心，使她不禁落淚，
　站在異邦的谷田裏想着家；
　　就是這聲音常常
在失掉了的仙域裏引動窗扉：
　一個美女望着大海險惡的浪花⑵。

呵，失掉了！這句話好比一聲鐘
　使我猛省到我站脚的地方！
別了！幻想，這騙人的妖童，
　不能老耍弄它盛傳的伎倆。
別了！別了！你怨訴的歌聲
　流過草坪，越過幽靜的溪水，
　　溜上山坡；而此時，它正深深
　　　埋在附近的谿谷中：
噫，這是個幻覺，還是夢寐？
　那歌聲去了：——我是睡？是醒？

　　　　　　　　　　　　查良錚譯

得到財寶和古堡中的公主為妻。這裏的詩句表示，夜鶯的歌會引動美人打開窗戶，遙望並期待她的騎士來援救她脫離險境。

223

59 Ode on a Grecian Urn

John Keats

Thou still unravish'd bride of quietness,
   Thou foster-child of silence and slow time,
Sylvan historian, who canst thus express
   A flowery tale more sweetly than our rhyme:
What leaf-fring'd legend haunts about thy shape
     Of deities or mortals, or of both,
        In Tempe or the dales of Arcady?
     What men or gods are these? What maidens loth?
What mad pursuit? What struggle to escape?
       What pipes and timbrels? What wild ecstasy?

Heard melodies are sweet, but those unheard
   Are sweeter; therefore, ye soft pipes, play on;
Not to the sensual ear, but, more endear'd,
   Pipe to the spirit ditties of no tone:
Fair youth, beneath the trees, thou canst not leave
     Thy song, nor ever can those trees be bare;
     Bold Lover, never, never canst thou kiss,
Though winning near the goal — yet, do not grieve;
     She cannot fade, though thou hast not thy bliss,

五十九　希臘古甕頌

約翰・濟慈

你委身"寂靜"的、完美的處子，
　　受過了"沉默"和"悠久"的撫育，
呵，田園的史家，你竟能鋪叙
　　一個如花的故事，比詩還瑰麗：
在你的形體上，豈非繚繞着
　　古老的傳說，以綠葉爲其邊緣；
　　　　講着人，或神，敦陂或阿卡狄(1)？
呵，是怎樣的人，或神！在舞樂前
多熱烈的追求！少女怎樣地逃躲！
　　　　怎樣的風笛和鼓鐃！怎樣的狂喜！

聽見的樂聲雖好，但若聽不見
　　却更美；所以，吹吧，柔情的風笛；
不是奏給耳朵聽，而是更甜，
　　它給靈魂奏出無聲的樂曲；
樹下的美少年呵，你無法中斷
　　你的歌，那樹木也落不了葉子；
　　　　鹵莽的戀人，你永遠、永遠吻不上，
雖然夠接近了——但不必心酸；
　　　　她不會老，雖然你不能如願以償，

---

(1)敦陂，古希臘西沙裏的山谷，以風景優美著稱。阿
　卡狄山谷也是牧歌中常歌頌的樂園。

For ever wilt thou love, and she be fair!

Ah, happy, happy boughs! that cannot shed
   Your leaves, nor ever bid the Spring adieu;
And, happy melodist, unwearied,
   For ever piping songs for ever new;
More happy love! more happy, happy love!
   For ever warm and still to be enjoy'd,
      For ever panting, and for ever young;
All breathing human passion far above,
   That leaves a heart high-sorrowful and cloy'd,
      A burning forehead, and a parching tongue.

Who are these coming to the sacrifice?
   To what green altar, O mysterious priest,
Lead'st thou that heifer lowing at the skies,
   And all her silken flanks with garlands drest?
What little town by river or sea shore,
   Or mountain-built with peaceful citadel,
      Is emptied of its folk, this pious morn?
And, little town, thy streets for evermore
   Will silent be; and not a soul to tell
      Why thou art desolate, can e'er return.

O Attic shape, fair attitude! with brede
   Of marble men and maidens overwrought,

　　　　你將永遠愛下去,她也永遠秀麗!

呵,幸福的樹木!你的枝葉
　　不會剝落,從不曾離開春天;
幸福的吹笛人也不會停歇,
　　他的歌曲永遠是那麼新鮮;
呵,更為幸福的、幸福的愛!
　　永遠熱烈,正等待情人宴饗,
　　　　永遠熱情地心跳,永遠年輕;
幸福的是這一切超凡的情態:
　　它不會使心靈饜足和悲傷,
　　　　沒有熾熱的頭腦,焦渴的嘴唇。

這些人是誰呵,都去赴祭祀?
　　這作犧牲的小牛,對天鳴叫,
你要牽它到哪兒,神秘的祭司?
　　花環綴滿着它光滑的身腰。
是從哪個傍河傍海的小鎮,
　　或哪個靜靜的堡寨的山村,
　　　　來了這些人,在這敬神的清早?
呵,小鎮,你的街道永遠恬靜;
　　再也不可能回來一個靈魂
　　　　告訴人你何以是這麼寂寥。

哦,希臘的形狀!唯美的觀照!
　　上面綴有石雕的男人和女人,

With forest branches and the trodden weed;
    Thou, silent form! dost tease us out of thought
As doth eternity: Cold Pastoral!
    When old age shall this generation waste
        Thou shalt remain, in midst of other woe
Than ours, a friend to man, to whom thou say'st,
'Beauty is Truth, Truth Beauty,' — that is all
    Ye know on earth, and all ye need to know.

還有林木,和踐踏過的青草;
　　沉默的形體呵,你像是"永恒"
使人超越思想:呵,冰冷的牧歌!
等暮年使這一世代都凋落,
　　只有你如舊;在另外的一些
憂傷中,你會撫慰後人說:
"美即是眞,眞即是美,"這就包括
　　你們所知道、和該知道的一切。

　　　　　　　　　　　　　查良錚譯

60 La Belle Dame sans Merci

John Keats

"O what can ail thee, knight-at-arms,
    Alone and palely loitering?
The sedge is wither'd from the lake,
    And no birds sing.

"O what can ail thee, knight-at-arms,
    So haggard and so woe-begone?
The squirrel's granary is full,
    And the harvest's done.

"I see a lily on thy brow
    With anguish moist and fever dew;
And on thy cheek a fading rose
    Fast withereth too."

"I met a lady in the meads,
    Full beautiful — a faery's child,
Her hair was long, her foot was light,
    And her eyes were wild.

"I made a garland for her head,
    And bracelets too, and fragrant zone;
She look'd at me as she did love,

六十　無情的妖女

約翰・濟慈

騎士呵，是什麼苦惱你，
　　獨自沮喪地遊蕩？
湖中的蘆葦已經枯了，
　　也沒有鳥兒歌唱！

騎士呵，是什麼苦惱你，
　　這般憔悴和悲傷？
松鼠的小巢貯滿食物，
　　莊稼也都進了穀倉。

你的額角白似百合
　　垂掛着熱病的露珠，
你的面頰像是玫瑰，
　　正在很快地凋枯。——

我在草坪上遇見了
　　一個妖女，美似天仙，
她輕捷、長髮，而眼裏
　　野性的光芒閃閃。

我給她編織過花冠、
　　芬芳的腰帶和手鐲，
她柔聲地輕輕嘆息，

And made sweet moan.

"I set her on my pacing steed
   And nothing else saw all day long,
For sideways would she lean, and sing
    A faery's song.

"She found me roots of relish sweet,
   And honey wild and manna dew,
And sure in language strange she said,
    'I love thee true!'

"She took me to her elfin grot,
   And there she wept and sigh'd full sore;
And there I shut her wild, wild eyes
    With kisses four.

"And there she lullèd me asleep,
   And there I dream'd — Ah! woe betide!
The latest dream I ever dream'd
    On the cold hill's side.

"I saw pale kings and princes too,
   Pale warriors, death-pale were they all;
Who cried — La belle Dame sans Merci
    Hath thee in thrall!'

彷彿是真心愛我。

我帶她騎在駿馬上，
　　她把臉兒側對着我，
我整日什麼都不顧，
　　只聽她的妖女之歌。

她給採來美味的草根、
　　野蜜、甘露和仙果，
她用了一篇奇異的話，
　　說她是真心愛我。

她帶我到了她的山洞，
　　又是落淚，又是悲嘆，
我在那兒四次吻着
　　她野性的、野性的眼。

我被她迷得睡着了，
　　呵，做了個驚心的噩夢！
我看見國王和王子
　　也在那妖女的洞中，

還有無數的騎士，
　　都蒼白得像是骷髏；
他們叫道：無情的妖女
　　已把你作了俘囚！

"I saw their starved lips in the gloam
    With horrid warning gapèd wide,
And I awoke and found me here
    On the cold hill's side.

"And this is why I sojourn here
    Alone and palely loitering,
Though the sedge is wither'd from the lake,
    And no birds sing."

在幽暗裏，他們的癟嘴
　　大張着，預告着災禍；
我一覺醒來，看見自己
　　躺在這冰冷的山坡。

因此，我就留在這兒，
　　獨自沮喪地遊蕩；
雖然湖中的蘆葦已枯，
　　也沒有鳥兒歌唱。

　　　　　　　　　　　　　　查良錚譯

61 The Grasshopper and the Cricket

John Keats

The poetry of earth is never dead.
   When all the birds are faint with the hot sun
   And hide in cooling trees, a voice will run
From hedge to hedge about the new-mown mead —
That is the Grasshopper's. He takes the lead
   In summer luxury; he has never done
   With his delights, for when tired out with fun
He rests at ease beneath some pleasant weed.
The poetry of earth is ceasing never.
   On a lone winter evening, when the frost
      Has wrought a silence, from the stove there shrills
The cricket's song, in warmth increasing ever,
   And seems to one in drowsiness half lost,
      The grasshopper's among some grassy hills.

六十一　蝈蝈與蟋蟀

約翰·濟慈

大地富詩意，綿綿無盡期：
日炎鳥倦鳴，林蔭且棲息。
竹籬繞綠茵，芳草新刈齊；
其中忽有聲，繞籬悠悠起——
原是蝈蝈歌，歡樂渠爲首；
　仲夏多繁茂，泛若不繫舟，
　享之不能盡，歌來不知愁；
偶然有倦意，野草叢中休。
大地富詩意，綿綿永不息：
　冬夜洵淒淸，霜天多岑寂，
　　此時有灶爐，火燄暖人心。
蟋蟀乘雅興，引吭吐妙音；
　主人嗒然坐，似眠又似醒，
　　莫非蝈蝈歌，來自遠山靑。

孟光裕譯
孫　梁校

62 The Song of the Shirt

Thomas Hood

With fingers weary and worn,
  With eyelids heavy and red,
A Woman sat, in unwomanly rags,
  Plying her needle and thread —
    Stitch! stitch! stitch!
In poverty, hunger, and dirt,
And still with a voice of dolorous pitch
She sang the "Song of the Shirt!"

"Work! work! work!
While the cock is crowing aloof!
  And work — work — work,
Till the stars shine through the roof!
It's O! to be a slave
  Along with the barbarous Turk,
Where woman has never a soul to save,
  If this is Christian work!

"Work — work — work

霍特（1799—1845），生於倫敦。父親是書商，
由於經營失利，家庭陷入困境。霍特只讀了九年書，
便向報刊(特別是幽默雜誌)投稿謀生。他不僅寫詩和

六十二 襯衫之歌

托馬斯·霍特

手指又酸又痛，
眼皮又紅又重。
一個婦女坐着，
破衣不蔽體，
針綫不停息。——
　縫呀！縫呀！縫呀！
　貧窮，饑餓，骯髒，
　低唱襯衫歌，
　字字盡憂傷！

幹活！幹活！幹活！
遙聞雄鷄長鳴。
還得幹活——幹活——幹活，
直到曉星穿過屋頂。
　假如這是基督徒幹的活，
　啊！倒不如去做奴隸，
　侍候粗野的土耳其人；
　縱然這婦人死後不能去見上帝。

幹活——幹活——幹活——，

雜文，作漫畫，並從事雕刻。詩歌創作包括 *The Plea of the Midsummer Fairies, The Bridge of Sighs.*

Till the brain begins to swim;
    Work — work — work
Till the eyes are heavy and dim!
Seam, and gusset, and band,
    Band, and gusset, and seam,
Till over the buttons I fall asleep,
    And sew them on in a dream!

"O! Men with Sisters dear!
    O! Men! with Mothers and Wives!
It is not linen you're wearing out,
    But human creatures' lives!
    Stitch — stitch — stitch,
    In poverty, hunger, and dirt,
Sewing at once, with a double thread,
    A Shroud as well as a Shirt.

"But why do I talk of Death?
    That Phantom of grisly bone,
I hardly fear his terrible shape,
    It seems so like my own —
    It seems so like my own,
    Because of the fasts I keep,
Oh! God! that bread should be so dear,
    And flesh and blood so cheap!

幹到頭兒在發暈；
幹活——幹活——幹活,
幹到眼睛又澀又昏。
　　縫縫綴綴,邊邊角角,
　　邊邊角角,縫縫綴綴;
　　直到撲上鈕扣睡着了,
　　夢裏也在把鈕扣縫綴。

啊,有姐有妹的男子漢,
啊,有娘有妻的男子漢,
你們穿破的不是布,
而是生命的傷殘!
　　縫呀——縫呀——縫呀,
　　貧窮、饑餓,骯髒,
　　兩股綫,同時縫,
　　一身壽服,一件襯衫。

爲啥我要說到死亡?
骷髏架子幽靈晃;
那駭人的模樣我們不怕,
看來和我一個樣。
　　看來和我一個樣,
　　因我一直在齋戒。
　　啊,上帝,麵包何等珍貴,
　　血肉如此廉賤!

"Work — work — work!
   My labour never flags;
And what are its wages? A bed of straw,
   A crust of bread — and rags.
That shatter'd roof, — and this naked floor —
   A table — a broken chair —
And a wall so blank, my shadow I thank
   For sometimes falling there!

"Work — work — work!
From weary chime to chime,
   Work — work — work —
As prisoners work for crime!
   Band, and gusset, and seam,
   Seam, and gusset, and band,
Till the heart is sick, and the brain benumb'd,
   As well as the weary hand.

"Work — work — work,
In the dull December light,
   And work — work — work,
When the weather is warm and bright —
While underneath the eaves
   The brooding swallows cling
As if to show me their sunny backs
   And twit me with the spring.

幹活——幹活——幹活!
我的話沒完沒了。
工錢是什麼?一塊麵包皮,
一身破爛,一床稻草,
　一張粗桌,一把破椅,
　泥土的地,搖幌的屋頂;
　感謝牆壁的光禿,
　不時映上我的瘦影。

幹活——幹活——幹活!
微弱鐘聲遍遍催。
幹活——幹活——幹活!
就像囚犯服苦役。
　縫縫連連,邊邊角角,
　邊邊角角,縫縫連連,
　直到心兒慌,頭兒痲,
　手兒疲軟難抽綫。

幹活——幹活——幹活,
臘月天色陰沉沉;
還是幹活——幹活——幹活,
天氣轉暖日光明。
　簷下燕子築新巢,
　育雛抱卵亦辛勞,
　羽背陽光堪炫耀。
　我怎不知春來到?

243

"Oh! but to breathe the breath
Of the cowslip and primrose sweet —
   With the sky above my head,
And the grass beneath my feet,
For only one short hour
   To feel as I used to feel,
Before I knew the woes of want
   And the walk that costs a meal!

"Oh but for one short hour!
   A respite however brief!
No blessed leisure for Love or Hope,
   But only time for Grief!
A little weeping would ease my heart,
   But in their briny bed
My tears must stop, for every drop
   Hinders needle and thread!"

[Seam, and gusset, and band,
Band, and gusset, and seam,
   Work, work, work,
Like the Engine that works by Steam!
A mere machine of iron and wood
   That toils for Mammon's sake —
Without a brain to ponder and craze

哦，且去吐納立金花的香氣，
報春花的甜意；
瞧，腳下綠油油的青草，
頭上碧藍碧藍的蒼天；
　　只消短短一個小時，
　　往日感受重又回味；
　　莫待明白貧乏苦，
　　一餐果腹豈容易！

哦，只用短短一小時，
換換空氣夠匆忙。
片刻偷閒並非福，
時時悔恨又徬徨。
　　啜泣能使心意平，
　　眼中淚水仍須停；
　　若任淚水流，
　　針綫爲阻留！

邊邊，角角、條條，
縫縫，綴綴、拼拼。
幹活——幹活——幹活，
活像蒸汽推動的引擎。
　　道道地地的鐵木機器，
　　爲財神鞠躬又盡瘁。
　　沒有頭腦去冥思遙想，

Or a heart to feel — and break!]

With fingers weary and worn,
   With eyelids heavy and red,
A Woman sate in unwomanly rags,
   Plying her needle and thread —
     Stitch! stitch! stitch!
   In poverty, hunger, and dirt,
And still with a voice of dolorous pitch,
Would that its tone could reach the Rich! —
   She sang this "Song of the Shirt!"

也沒有心去感受——去破碎。

——手指又酸又痛,
　　眼皮又紅又重;
　　一個婦女坐着,
　　破衣不蔽體,
　　針綫不停息。——
縫呀!縫呀!縫呀!
貧窮,饑餓,骯髒,
低唱襯衫歌,
音意何哀傷!
但願此曲傳入朱門與華堂!

吳漢文譯
孫　梁校

63 The Apology

Ralph Waldo Emerson

Think me not unkind and rude
    That I walk alone in grove and glen;
I go to the god of the wood
    To fetch his word to men.

Tax not my sloth that I
    Fold my arms beside the brook;
Each cloud that floated in the sky
    Writes a letter in my book.

Chide me not, laborious hand,
    For the idle flowers I brought;
Every aster in my hand
    Goes home loaded with a thought.

There was never mystery
    But 't is figured in the flowers;
Was never secret history
    But birds tell it in the bowers.

埃默生(1803—1882),生於美國波士頓,曾任北方教會牧師,後因反對傳統的清規戒律而退職。1832年遊歷歐洲時,結識沃茲沃斯、柯爾律奇與卡萊爾。

六十三　辯　白

拉爾夫・華爾多・埃默生

莫認爲我孤僻粗魯，
獨自在叢林幽谷漫步；
我去拜謁樹林之神，
把他的話傳給凡夫。

莫責備我懶散，
在溪畔抱着雙臂；
天上飄浮的每朵雲彩，
一一寫進我的書裏。

辛勤的人們，莫責怪我
採擷無用的花朵；
我手中的每朵紫菀
隨我歸家，妙思寄托。

凡是神秘的事物，
都由鮮花勾畫形象；
凡是隱秘的事蹟，
都由鳥兒在林蔭歌唱。

埃默生以散文作品著稱，詩作有《詩集》(*Poems*)、《代表人物》(*Representative Men*)、《英國人的特性》(*English Traits*)等。

One harvest from thy field
    Homeward brought the oxen strong;
A second crop thine acres yield,
    Which I gather in a song.

你田裏的第一次收穫，
由健壯的牛載回家去；
你地裏長的第二批莊稼，
我把它譜成歌曲。

楊　霖譯
孫　梁校

64 Sonnets from the Portuguese: I

Elizabeth Barret Browning

I thought once how Theocritus had sung
   Of the sweet years, the dear and wished-for years,
   Who each one in a gracious hand appears
To bear a gift for mortals, old or young:
And, as I mused it in his antique tongue,
   I saw, in gradual vision through my tears,
   The sweet, sad years, the melancholy years,
Those of my own life, who by turns had flung
A shadow across me. Straightway I was 'ware,
   So weeping, how a mystic Shape did move
Behind me, and drew me backward by the hair;
   And a voice said in mastery, while I strove, . . .
"Guess now who holds thee?" — "Death," I said. But there,
   The silver answer rang, . . . "Not Death, but Love."

白朗寧夫人（1806—1861），十五歲時弄傷了脊骨，直至婚前不久才漸告康服。1850年出版《葡萄牙十四行詩集》(*Sonnets from the Portugese*)，1856

六十四　抒情十四行詩選：一

伊麗莎白・巴萊特・白朗寧

我想起昔年那位希臘的詩人[1]，
唱着流年的歌兒——可愛的流年，
渴望中的流年，一個個的宛然
都手執着頒送給世人的禮品：
我沈吟着詩人的古調，我不禁
淚眼發花了，於是我漸漸看見
那溫柔淒切的流年，酸苦的流年，
我自己的流年，輪流擲着暗影，
掠過我的身邊。馬上我哭起來，
我明知道有一個神秘的模樣，
在背後揪着我的頭髮往後掇，
正在掙扎的當兒，我聽見好像
一個厲聲："誰掇着你，猜猜！"
"死，"我說。"不是死，是愛，"他講。

聞一多譯

年再版時補添一首，共四十四首。
[1]指狄奧克里塔斯（Theocritus），公元前三世紀希臘詩人，西方田園詩的創始者，影響深遠。

65 Sonnets from the Portuguese: III

Elizabeth Barret Browning

Unlike are we, unlike, O princely Heart!
   Unlike our uses and our destinies.
   Our ministering two angels look surprise
On one another, as they strike athwart
Their wings in passing. Thou, bethink thee, art
   A guest for queens to social pageantries,
   With gages from a hundred brighter eyes
Than tears even can make mine, to play thy part
Of chief musician. What hast thou to do
   With looking from the lattice-lights at me —
A poor, tired, wandering singer, singing through
   The dark, and leaning up a cypress tree?
   The chrism is on thine head — on mine the dew —
And Death must dig the level where these agree.

六十五　抒情十四行詩選：三

伊麗莎白·巴萊特·白朗寧

我們原不一樣，尊貴的人兒呀，
原不一樣是我們的職司與前程。
你我的主管的天使迎面飛來，
翅膀碰上了翅膀，大家瞪着
驚愕的眼睛。你想，你是華宮裏
后妃的上賓，千百雙殷勤的明眸
（我的眼，縱然掛滿了淚珠，也不能教我
勝過這光彩）請求你主掌歌班。
那你幹什麼從那燈光輝映的窗子裏
望向我？——我，一個淒楚流浪的
歌者，疲憊地靠着柏樹(1)，吟歎在
茫茫的黑暗裏。聖油搽在你頭上(2)——
我頭上承受着涼透的夜露。
只有死，才能把這樣的一對扯個平。

方平譯

---

(1)西洋習俗，常以柏樹枝對死者表示哀悼。
(2)舉行加冕禮時，先在帝王頭上搽油，然後加冕。

66 A Psalm of Life

Henry Wadsworth Longfellow

Tell me not in mournful numbers,
    Life is but an empty dream!
For the soul is dead that slumbers,
    And things are not what they seem.

Life is real! Life is earnest!
    And the grave is not its goal;
Dust thou art, to dust returnest,
    Was not spoken of the soul.

Not enjoyment, and not sorrow,
    Is our destined end or way;
But to act, that each to-morrow
    Finds us farther than to-day.

Art is long, and Time is fleeting,
    And our hearts, though stout and brave,
Still, like muffled drums, are beating
    Funeral marches to the grave.

    朗費羅（1807—1882），生於美國波特蘭，1836至1854年間任哈佛大學現代語言教授。朗費羅的主要作品有抒情詩集《夜籟》（*Voices of the Night*）、

六十六 生之讚歌

亨利・瓦茨沃斯・朗費羅

莫唱傷感調：
夢幻是人生！
須知靈魂睡，
所見本非眞。

生命眞而誠！
墳墓非止境；
生死皆垢塵，
豈是指靈魂。

逸樂與憂傷，
均非天行健；
君子當自強，
翌日勝今天。

光陰似白駒，
學藝垂千秋；
雄心如悶鼓，
葬曲伴荒丘。

《邁爾斯・司坦廸希求婚記》(*The Courtship of Miles Standish*)、《伊凡傑蘭》(*Evangeline*)、《海華沙之歌》(*The Song of Hiawatha*)等。

In the world's broad field of battle,
    In the bivouac of Life,
Be not like dumb, driven cattle!
    Be a hero in the strife!

Trust no Future, howe'er pleasant!
    Let the dead Past bury its dead!
Act — act in the living Present!
    Heart within, and God o'erhead!

Lives of great men all remind us
    We can make our lives sublime,
And, departing, leave behind us
    Footprints on the sands of time;

Footprints that perhaps another,
    Sailing o'er life's solemn main,
A forlorn and shipwrecked brother,
    Seeing, shall take heart again.

Let us, then, be up and doing,
    With a heart for any fate;
Still achieving, still pursuing,
    Learn to labour and to wait.

世界一戰場，
人生一軍營；
莫效牛馬走，
奮發斯英雄！

莫信未來好，
過去任埋葬。
努力有生時，
心誠祈上蒼！

偉人洵不朽，
我亦能自強，
鴻爪留身後，
遺澤印時光。

或有飄零人，
苦海中浮沉，
覩我足印時，
衷心又振奮。

衆生齊奮發，
順逆不介意；
勤勉而戒躁，
探索又進取。

蘇仲翔譯
孫　梁校

67 My Lost Youth

Henry Wadsworth Longfellow

Often I think of the beautiful town
    That is seated by the sea;
Often in thought go up and down
The pleasant streets of that dear old town,
    And my youth comes back to me.
        And a verse of a Lapland song
        Is haunting my memory still:
        "A boy's will is the wind's will,
And the thoughts of youth are long, long thoughts."

I can see the shadowy lines of its trees,
    And catch, in sudden gleams,
The sheen of the far-surrounding seas,
And islands that were the Hesperides
    Of all my boyish dreams.
        And the burden of that old song,
        It murmurs and whispers still:
        "A boy's will is the wind's will,
And the thoughts of youth are long, long thoughts."

I remember the black wharves and the slips,

六十七 我失去的青春

亨利・瓦茨沃斯・朗費羅

我常常想到那美麗的小城(1)，
　　它就座落在海岸；
我常常幻想走進那古老的小城，
在它快樂的街道上來回步行，
　　於是青春又回到我身邊。
　　　那北歐歌謠裏的一句話
　　　仍舊在我的記憶裏迴蕩：
　　"少年的願望好似風的願望，
呵，青春的心思是多麼、多麼綿長。"

我能看見小城參差的樹影，
　　我眼前還忽而掠過
環抱它的海上遠遠閃來的光明
和一列島嶼（它們為少年的夢
　　作了樂園的守護者）。
　　　那支古老的歌的叠唱
　　　仍舊在對我低語、傾訴：
　　"少年的願望好似風的願望，
呵，青春的心思是多麼、多麼綿長。"

我記得那烏黑的碼頭和停泊地，

---

(1)指作者的故鄉波特蘭。

  And the sea-tides tossing free;
And Spanish sailors with bearded lips,
And the beauty and mystery of the ships,
  And the magic of the sea.
    And the voice of that wayward song
    Is singing and saying still:
    "A boy's will is the wind's will,
And the thoughts of youth are long, long thoughts."

I remember the bulwarks by the shore,
  And the fort upon the hill;
The sunrise gun, with its hollow roar,
The drum-beat repeated o'er and o'er,
  And the bugle wild and shrill.
    And the music of that old song
    Throbs in my memory still:
    "A boy's will is the wind's will,
And the thoughts of youth are long, long thoughts."

I remember the sea-fight far away,
  How it thundered o'er the tide!
And the dead captains, as they lay

和海濤的自由奔騰,
還有西班牙的水手留着髭鬚,
還有船隻的可愛和神秘,
　　大海是這般迷人!
　　　那一段固執的歌聲
　　　　仍舊在訴說和振蕩:
　"少年的願望好似風的願望,
呵,青春的心思是多麼、多麼綿長。"

我記得海邊和山上的碉堡;
　在太陽初昇的時候,
傳過來大砲低沉的咆哮,
鼓也在不停地咚咚地敲,
　　號聲壯闊而又顫抖。
　　　那古老的歌的音調
　　　　仍舊在我的心裏激蕩:
　"少年的願望好似風的願望,
呵,青春的心思是多麼、多麼綿長。"

我記得戰爭⑴在遠方的海上
　轟隆之聲傳過了水面!
我記得如何埋葬了戰死的船長,

⑴指1813年9月美國海船"進取號"和英國海船"拳擊家號"在波特樂港外的交戰,兩艘船的船長都戰死,並葬於公共墓地。

In their graves, o'erlooking the tranquil bay
   Where they in battle died.
      And the sound of that mournful song
      Goes through me with a thrill:
      "A boy's will is the wind's will,
And the thoughts of youth are long, long thoughts."

I can see the breezy dome of groves,
   The shadows of Deering's Woods;
And the friendships old and the early loves
Come back with a Sabbath sound, as of doves
   In quiet neighbourhoods.
      And the verse of that sweet old song,
      It flutters and murmurs still:
      "A boy's will is the wind's will,
And the thoughts of youth are long, long thoughts."

I remember the gleams and glooms that dart
   Across the school-boy's brain;
The song and the silence in the heart,
That in part are prophecies, and in part
   Are longings wild and vain.
      And the voice of that fitful song
      Sings on, and is never still:

他們的墳墓就對着他們的戰場——
　　那一片寂靜的海灣。
　　　那悲哀之歌的音響
　　　痛楚地刺過了我的心：
　　"少年的願望好似風的願望，
呵，青春的心思是多麼、多麼綿長。"

我能看見輕風拂着叢林的圓頂，
　　和狄嶺(1)森林的蔭翳；
於是舊日的友誼和青春的戀情
帶着安息的樂音流往我心中，
　　像是鴿子迴旋在寂靜裏。
　　　那甜蜜的古老的歌辭
　　　仍舊在起伏和低唱：
　　"少年的願望好似風的願望，
呵，青春的心思是多麼、多麼綿長。"

我記得那掠過學童的腦海的
　　閃爍的光亮和幽暗；
我記得有過心靈的歌唱和沉寂，
一半是預言，一半是熱狂的
　　枉然的追求與夢幻。
　　　而那任性的歌仍舊
　　　唱下去，仍舊在波蕩：

─────────

(1)狄嶺，美國緬因州的一個小城，在作者的故鄉波特
　蘭附近。

>   "A boy's will is the wind's will,
> And the thoughts of youth are long, long thoughts."

There are things of which I may not speak;
   There are dreams that cannot die;
There are thoughts that make the strong heart weak,
And bring a pallor into the cheek,
   And a mist before the eye.
      And the words of that fatal song
      Come over me like a chill:
      "A boy's will is the wind's will,
And the thoughts of youth are long, long thoughts."

Strange to me now are the forms I meet
   When I visit the dear old town;
But the native air is pure and sweet,
And the trees that o'ershadow each well-known street,
   As they balance up and down,
      Are singing the beautiful song,
      Are sighing and whispering still:
      "A boy's will is the wind's will,
And the thoughts of youth are long, long thoughts."

And Deering's Woods are fresh and fair,
   And with joy that is almost pain
My heart goes back to wander there,

"少年的願望好似風的願望,
呵,青春的心思是多麼、多麼綿長。"

有一些事物我不想再傾吐;
　有一些夢想從不死去;
有一些懷念使心靈變為脆弱,
它會給面頰帶來蒼白的顏色,
　使眼睛感到模糊。
　　那致命的歌的一句話
　　　像一陣冷氣撲到我心上:
　"少年的願望好似風的願望,
呵,青春的心思是多麼、多麼綿長。"

我在那古老的小城所見的形體
　如今已顯得陌生,
但鄉土的空氣確是純潔而甜蜜,
而那蔭蔽每條熟悉的街道的
　樹木,當它們來回擺動,
　　就唱出一支美麗的歌,
　　這歌曲仍在歎息和低唱:
　"少年的願望好似風的願望,
呵,青春的心思是多麼、多麼綿長。"

狄嶺森林幽靜、新鮮而美麗,
　我的心懷着一種
近似痛楚的快樂飛回到那裏,

And among the dreams of the days that were,
   I find my lost youth again.
      And the strange and beautiful song,
      The groves are repeating it still:
      "A boy's will is the wind's will,
And the thoughts of youth are long, long thoughts."

而當我縈迴於那往日的夢迹,
　我又找到失去的青春。
　　那奇異而美麗的歌,
　　在樹林裏發出了回響:
　"少年的願望好似風的願望,
呵,青春的心思是多麼、多麼綿長。"

　　　　　　　　　　　查良錚譯

68 The Arrow and the Song

Henry Wadsworth Longfellow

I shot an arrow into the air,
It fell to earth, I knew not where;
For, so swiftly it flew, the sight
Could not follow it in its flight.

I breathed a song into the air,
It fell to earth, I knew not where;
For who has sight so keen and strong,
That it can follow the flight of song?

Long, long afterwards, in an oak
I found the arrow, still unbroke;
And the song, from beginning to end,
I found again in the heart of a friend.

六十八　箭和歌

亨利·瓦茨沃斯·朗費羅

我射一箭直上高空，
待它落下，不見影踪；
因為它飛得如此疾迅，
我的眼力無法追尋。

我歌一曲響遏行雲，
待它飄下，無處覓尋；
誰的眼力那麼強，
能追隨歌聲飛揚？

好久、好久後，我見一株橡樹，
樹上嵌着箭，完好如故；
那首歌，從頭至尾，我也發現
在一位友人深深的心田。

楊　霖譯

孫　梁校

69 The Golden Sunset

Henry Wadsworth Longfellow

The golden sea its mirror spread
  Beneath the golden skies,
And but a narrow strip between
  Of land and shadow lies.

The cloud-like rocks, the rock-like clouds
  Dissolved in glory float,
And midway of the radiant flood,
  Hangs silently the boat.

The sea is but another sky,
  The sky a sea as well,
And which is earth and which is heaven,
  The eye can scarcely tell.

So when for us life's evening hour,
  Soft fading shall descend,
May glory, born of earth and heaven,
  The earth and heaven blend.

Flooded with peace the spirits float,
  With silent rapture glow,

六十九　金色夕照

亨利・瓦茨沃斯・朗費羅

波平似鏡，映照天宇，
　水天金色一片。
彼岸隱現，雲影緩移，
　遙望依稀一綫。

岩如行雲，雲如巉岩，
　化作異彩飄浮；
波光瀲灩；注目中流：
　凝泊一葉扁舟。

茫茫然蒼天如大海，
　浩浩然大海似蒼天；
何處天上？何處人間？
　俗眼豈能分辨?!

因而在人生暮年，
　桑榆之景隱現時，
願天地孕育的光華
　將天地溶爲一體。

心靈洋溢着寧謐，
　在沉靜的欣悅中升華；

Till where earth ends and heaven begins,
　The soul shall scarcely know.

性靈與天地交融，
不分何處天上何處地下。

孫　梁譯

70 Annabel Lee

Edgar Allan Poe

It was many and many a year ago,
   In a kingdom by the sea,
That a maiden there lived whom you may know
   By the name of Annabel Lee;
And this maiden she lived with no other thought
   Than to love and be loved by me.

She was a child and *I* was a child,
   In this kingdom by the sea,
But we loved with a love that was more than love —
   I and my Annabel Lee —
With a love that the winged seraphs of Heaven
   Coveted her and me.

And this was the reason that, long ago,
   In this kingdom by the sea,
A wind blew out of a cloud by night
   Chilling my Annabel Lee;

    阿侖・坡（1809—1849），西方推理小說和恐怖小說的先驅者，生於美國波士頓。1836年與表妹弗吉尼亞・克萊姆（Virginia Clemm）結婚。十年後妻子患肺結核去世，阿侖・坡悲慟欲絕，以致精神失常。生前曾出版詩集《帖木耳》（*Tamerlane*）、《艾爾・

七十　安娜貝·李

埃特加·阿侖·坡

那是多年多年以前的事：
　　在海邊的一個王國裏，
有個姑娘你可能知道，
　　名字叫安娜貝·李。
她不懷有別的心思，
　　除了和我相愛相媅。

她是個孩子，我是個孩子，
　　在海邊的這個王國裏，
以一種超越愛的愛而相愛；
　　我們——我和安娜貝·李，
以一種愛，長着六翼的天使
　　也對她和我艷羨不已。

正是這個原因，
　　在海濱的這個王國裏，
從雲端刮起一陣風，
　　冷徹美麗的安娜貝·李；

阿拉夫》(*Al Aaraaf*)、《詩集》(*Poems*)等。

　《安娜貝·李》據說是詩人悼念亡妻之作，共分六節，每節中四音步與三音步的詩行交錯，並多叠句的手法，旋律極強。

So that her highborn kinsmen came
   And bore her away from me,
To shut her up in a sepulcher
   In this kingdom by the sea.

The angels, not half so happy in Heaven,
   Went envying her and me:
Yes! that was the reason (as all men know,
   In this kingdom by the sea)
That the wind came out of the cloud, chilling
   And killing my Annabel Lee.

But our love it was stronger by far than the love
   Of those who were older than we —
   Of many far wiser than we —
And neither the angels in Heaven above,
   Nor the demons down under the sea,
Can ever dissever my soul from the soul
   Of the beautiful Annabel Lee:

For the moon never beams without bringing me dreams
   Of the beautiful Annabel Lee;
And the stars never rise but I see the bright eyes
   Of the beautiful Annabel Lee;
And so, all the night-tide, I lie down by the side
Of my darling, my darling, my life and my bride,

她的高貴的親屬,
　　硬把我們拆散分離;
把她關進墓穴,
　　就在這海濱王國裏。

天使在天堂並不怎樣快樂,
　　他們對我倆心懷嫉忌。
正是!——正是這個緣由,
　　(衆所周知,就在這海濱王國裏,)
夜黑,雲暗,風起,
　　凍殺了我的安娜貝·李。

但直到如今,我們的愛更強,
　　比年長於我們的愛更深,
　　比智慧超過我們的愛更誠。
不是天上的天使,
　　也不是海底的妖精,
能拆散我們的魂靈——
　　我和美麗的安娜貝的魂靈。

因爲:每當月光輕籠,
　　便帶我進入美麗的安娜貝的夢境。
每當羣星升起,我便看見
　　美麗的安娜貝晶瑩的眼睛。
因此:漫漫長夜,我都躺在她的身邊,
　　——我的生命,我的愛人,我的新娘的身邊;

In the sepulcher there by the sea —
In her tomb by the side of the sea.

在海邊她的墓裏——
在滄海之濱的墳裏。

吳興祿譯
孫　梁校

71 The Rubáiyát of Omar Khayyám of Naishápúr (Extract)

Edward Fitzgerald

I

Wake! For the Sun, who scattered into flight
The Stars before him from the Field of Night,
    Drives Night along with them from Heav'n, and strikes
The Sultan's Turret with a Shaft of Light.

XII

A Book of Verses underneath the Bough,
A Jug of Wine, a Loaf of Bread — and Thou
    Beside me singing in the Wilderness —
Oh, Wilderness were Paradise enow!

XVII

Think, in this battered Caravanserai
Whose Portals are alternate Night and Day,
    How Sultán after Sultán with his Pomp
Abode his destined Hour, and went his way.

菲茲吉拉德(1809—1883),生於英國薩福克郡,
父姓本爲蒲舍爾(Purcell),父死後,改依母姓。
最著名作品爲英譯十一世紀波斯詩人莪默·伽亞謨

七十一 莪默·伽亞謨作《魯拜集》
（節選）

愛德華·菲茲吉拉德

一

醒呀！太陽驅散了羣星，
暗夜從空中逃遁，
燦爛的金箭，
射中了蘇丹的高瓴。

十二

樹蔭下放着一卷詩章，
一瓶葡萄美酒，一點乾糧，
有你在這荒原中傍我歡歌——
荒原呀，啊，便是天堂！

十七

天地是飄搖的逆旅，
晝夜是逆旅的門戶，
多少蘇丹與榮華，
住不多時，又匆匆離去。

（Omar Khayyám）所作的《魯拜集》（*Rubáiyát*）。
　　魯拜詩的形式爲一首四行，第一、二、四行押韻，第三行大抵不押韻。

XXVIII

With them the seed of Wisdom did I sow,
And with mine own hand wrought to make it grow;
   And this was all the Harvest that I reaped —
"I came like Water, and like Wind I go."

LXVIII

We are no other than a moving row
Of Magic Shadow-shapes that come and go
   Round with the Sun-illumined Lantern held
In Midnight by the Master of the Show;

LXXII

And that inverted Bowl they call the Sky,
Whereunder crawling cooped we live and die,
   Lift not your hands to *It* for help — for It
As impotently moves as you or I.

LXXVII

And this I know: whether the one True Light
Kindle to Love, or Wrath consume me quite,

二十八

我也學播了智慧之種，
親手培植它漸漸葱蘢；
而今我所獲得的收成——
只是"來如流水，逝如風。"

六十八

我們是活動的幻影之羣，
繞着這走馬燈兒來去，
在一個夜半深更，
點燃在魔術師的手裏。

七十二

人稱說天宇是個覆盆，
我們匍匐着在此生死，
莫用舉手去求他哀憐——
他之不能動移猶如我你。

七十七

我知道：無論是燃燒於情
或者是激怒灼焚我身，

One Flash of It within the Tavern caught
Better than in the Temple lost outright.

CI

And when like her, oh Sákí, you shall pass
Among the Guests Star-scattered on the Grass,
    And in your joyous errand reach the spot
Where I made One — turn down an empty Glass!

在這茅店內能捉得一閃"眞光"，
比在寺院中出家的優勝。

—〇—

啊，"釃客"⁽¹⁾哟！當你像那月兒
在星羅草上的羣客之中來往，
你釃到了我坐過的這個坐場
——你請爲我呀，祭奠一觴！

郭沫若譯

⑴ "釃客"（Saki）：波斯語，此言托盞者，比喻造化。

72 Break, Break, Break

Alfred Tennyson

Break, break, break,
 On thy cold grey stones, O Sea!
And I would that my tongue could utter
 The thoughts that arise in me.

O well for the fisherman's boy,
 That he shouts with his sister at play!
O well for the sailor lad,
 That he sings in his boat on the bay!

And the stately ships go on
 To their haven under the hill;
But O for the touch of a vanish'd hand,
 And the sound of a voice that is still!

Break, break, break,
 At the foot of thy crags, O Sea!
But the tender grace of a day that is dead
 Will never come back to me.

丹尼生(1809—1892),生於英國林肯郡,出身牧師家庭,兄弟均有詩才,早年曾合作出版詩集 *Poems by Two Brothers*。名作有《抒情詩集》(*Poems : Chiefly Lyrical*)、《悼亡詩——紀念漢勒姆》(*In Memoriam A.H.H.*)、《公主》(*The Princess*)、

七十二　拍岸曲

阿爾弗雷德·丹尼生

拍岸，拍岸，拍岸，
波濤拍擊灰岩；
思潮如泉湧，
但願能言宣。

美哉漁家子，
同姊妹嬉笑謔浪！
美哉船家子，
海灣內扁舟詠唱！

巍巍巨輪徐徐駛，
　駛入山麓港灣；
憶昔日纖手輕撫，
　喁喁絮語杳然！

拍岸，拍岸，拍岸，
洪濤拍擊巉岩！
柔情如水永不返，
惆悵思緒萬千。

　　　　　　　孫　梁譯

《毛特》(*Maud*)、《君王敘事組詩》(*Idylls of the King*)。

　《拍岸曲》以海邊景色襯托對往日戀情的追憶。

73 Crossing the Bar

Alfred Tennyson

Sunset and evening star,
   And one clear call for me!
And may there be no moaning of the bar,
   When I put out to sea,

But such a tide as moving seems asleep,
   Too full for sound and foam,
When that which drew from out the boundless deep
   Turns again home.

Twilight and evening bell,
   And after that the dark!
And may there be no sadness of farewell,
   When I embark;

For though from out our bourne of Time and Place
   The flood may bear me far,
I hope to see my Pilot face to face
   When I have crost the bar.

七十三　渡沙渚

阿爾弗雷德·丹尼生

夕陽下，閃疏星，
召喚一聲清朗！
願沙渚寧靜，
我將出海遠航；

潮汐如夢幻，
濤聲似止，浪花息；
大海深處湧來，
又悄然退却。

暮靄鐘鳴，
黑夜將籠罩！
願訣別無悲聲，
登舟起錨；

千古洪流，時空無限，
滔滔載我至遠方；
渡沙渚一綫，
泰然見領航[1]。

孫　梁譯

《渡沙渚》抒發了死神逼近時樂天知命的襟懷。
(1) 隱喩上帝。

74 Sweet and Low

Alfred Tennyson

Sweet and low, sweet and low,
Wind of the western sea,
Low, low, breathe and blow,
Wind of the western sea!
Over the rolling waters go,
Come from the dying moon, and blow,
Blow him again to me;
While my little one, while my pretty one, sleeps.

Sleep and rest, sleep and rest,
Father will come to thee soon;
Rest, rest on mother's breast,
Father will come to thee soon;
Father will come to his babe in the nest,
Silver sails all out of the west
Under the silver moon;
Sleep, my little one, sleep, my pretty one, sleep.

七十四　輕輕地，柔和地
阿爾弗雷特·丹尼生

輕輕地、柔和地，輕輕地、柔和地，
西方吹來海風；
輕輕地、輕輕地吹拂，
西方吹來海風！
西邊吹來，月色朦朧，
吹過波濤洶湧；
吹得他回家呵，
親親睡着的寶寶，可愛的寶貝。

睡吧，休息；睡吧，休息，
爸爸一會兒就來；
睡吧，睡在媽媽懷裏，
爸爸一會兒就來；
從西方歸來，揚起銀色風帆，
映着銀色月光，飄洋過海，
來看寶寶——安睡在家裏；
睡吧，小寶貝，睡吧，可愛的寶貝。

宗　白譯
孫　梁校

75 Home-Thoughts, from the Sea

Robert Browning

Nobly, nobly Cape Saint Vincent to the North-west died away;
Sunset ran, one glorious blood-red, reeking into Cadiz Bay;
Bluish 'mid the burning water, full in face Trafalgar lay;
In the dimmest North-east distance dawn'd Gibraltar grand and gray;
"Here and here did England help me: how can I help England?" — say,
Whoso turns as I, this evening, turn to God to praise and pray,
While Jove's planet rises yonder, silent over Africa.

　　白朗寧（1812—1889），生於倫敦，1846年與伊麗莎白·巴萊特結婚後，在意大利定居。白朗寧在詩歌中首創"戲劇性獨白"（dramatic monologue）的手法，主要作品有《戲劇抒情詩集》（*Dramatic Lyrics*）、《戲劇傳奇和抒情詩集》（*Dramatic Romances and Lyrics*）、《環與書》（*The Ring and the Book*）等。

　　《海上鄉思》和《海外鄉思》刊於詩集《鐘和石

七十五　海上鄉思

羅伯特・白朗寧

聖維森特角(1)巍巍然向西北隱沒，
紅日西沉，如華嚴光輪，向卡廸茲灣(2)旋落；
藍濛濛特拉法加(3)迎面聳峙，殷紅海水襯托，
渺渺然東北方隱現宏偉的直布羅陀(4)；
遙望非洲大陸，木星在天際默默閃爍，
此時人同此心，一齊讚美上帝而禱祝：
"祖國曾在此地爭光，我應如何盡忠報國！"

孫　梁譯

榴》(*Bells and Pomegranates*)。
(1)葡萄牙南方大西洋沿岸的海岬。
(2)在聖維森特角之東。這兩行表明詩人在海上由西向東航行。
(3)特拉法加在直布羅陀之西。1805年，英國海軍上將納爾遜(Horatio Nelson)在此擊敗拿破崙的海軍。
(4)西班牙與摩洛哥之間的戰略要地。

76 Home-Thoghts, from Abroad

Robert Browning

O to be in England
Now that April's there,
And whoever wakes in England
Sees, some morning, unaware,
That the lowest boughs and the brushwood sheaf
Round the elm-tree bole are in tiny leaf,
While the chaffinch sings on the orchard bough
In England — now!

And after April, when May follows,
And the whitethroat builds, and all the swallows!
Hark, where my blossom'd pear-tree in the hedge
Leans to the field and scatters on the clover
Blossoms and dewdrops — at the bent spray's edge —
That's the wise thrush; he sings each song twice over,
Lest you should think he never could recapture
The first fine careless rapture!

七十六　海外鄉思

羅伯特・白朗寧

郁郁英倫好，緬想四月初；
清晨夢乍醒，一碧吐新榆；
繁枝繞老樹，葉葉正扶疏；
婉囀金絲雀，歌喉美且腴；
英倫好時節，孟夏月清和！

翩翩忽五月，歸燕啄新泥；
籬畔玉梨開，田邊金花敷；
花葉低垂處，清露綴明珠；
畫眉啼不住，每歌意躊躇；
深恐再聽難，意外片歡愉。

蘇仲翔譯
孫　梁校

77 Pippa's Song

Robert Browning

The year's at the spring,
And day's at the morn;
Morning's at seven;
The hillside's dew-pearled;
The lark's on the wing;
The snail's on the thorn:
God's in His heaven —
All's right with the world!

七十七　比芭之歌

羅伯特・白朗寧

一年中早春，
一天中清晨，
早晨七點多清新；
山坡露珠閃光，
雲雀飛翔高空，
蝸牛歡喜蠕動；
上帝安居天堂——
世上一切順當！

宗　白譯
孫　梁校

《比芭之歌》爲詩劇《比芭經過》(*Pippa Passes*)中的一支插曲。比芭是劇中一個意大利青年女工，常在街頭漫步，唱着歌謠。

78 The Fountain

James Russell Lowell

Into the sunshine,
  Full of the light,
Leaping and flashing
  From morn till night!

Into the moonlight,
  Whiter than snow,
Waving so flower-like
  When the winds blow!

Into the starlight,
  Rushing in spray,
Happy at midnight,
  Happy by day.

Ever in motion,
  Blithesome and cheery,
Still climbing heavenward,
  Never aweary:

洛威爾(1819—1891),生於美國馬薩諸塞州,歷任哈佛大學現代語言教授,《大西洋月刊》(*Atlantic Monthly*)主編,美國駐西班牙及英國公使。主要作

七十八　噴　泉

詹姆斯・羅塞爾・洛威爾

射入日光，
　晶輝彌滿，
跳躍閃爍，
　從早至晚！

射入月光，
　純白逾雪，
如彼花開，
　隨風波屈！

射入星光，
　飛迸如霞，
夜半欣然。
　晝亦欣然。

常在動中，
　載愉載恬，
永欲摩天，
　不知疲倦；

品有長詩《為批評家所作寓言》(*A Fable for Critics*)、詩集《比格羅文存》(*Biglow Papers*)。
　《噴泉》以輕快節奏表現美國式樂觀精神。

Glad of all weathers,
   Still seeming best,
Upward or downward
   Motion thy rest;

Full of a nature
   Nothing can tame,
Changed every moment,
   Ever the same;

Ceaseless aspiring,
   Ceaseless content,
Darkness or sunshine
   Thy element;

Glorious fountain!
   Let my heart be
Fresh, changeful, constant,
   Upward like thee!

不分晴雨,
　　總覺歡樂,
頡之頏之,
　　動中休息;

精力充沛,
　　不屈不撓,
刻刻變化,
　　不改其操;

不斷亢揚,
　　不斷滿足,
無晝無夜,
　　一元太極;

燦哉噴泉,
　　我心榜樣,
新穎多變,
　　永恆向上!

　　　　　　　　　郭沫若譯

79 I Hear America Singing

Walt Whitman

I hear America singing, the varied carols I hear,
Those of mechanics, each one singing his as it should be blithe and strong,
The carpenter singing his as he measures his plank or beam,
The mason singing his as he makes ready for work, or leaves off work,
The boatman singing what belongs to him in his boat, the deckhand singing on the steamboat deck,
The shoemaker singing as he sits on his bench, the hatter singing as he stands,
The wood-cutter's song, the ploughboy's on his way in the morning, or at noon intermission or at sundown,
The delicious singing of the mother, or of the young wife at work, or of the girl sewing or washing,
Each singing what belongs to him or her and to none else,
The day what belongs to the day — at night the party of young fellows, robust, friendly,
Singing with open mouths their strong melodious songs.

七十九　我聽見美利堅在歌唱

瓦爾特·惠特曼

我聽見美利堅在歌唱，我聽見各種不同的歡歌，
機械工的歡歌，每人照例唱着他自己的歌，歌
　　聲快樂而健壯，
木工在裁量他的木板或橫樑時唱着他的歌，
瓦工在準備上工或歇工時唱着他的歌，
船夫唱着他船上自己所有的一切，艙面水手在
　　輪船的甲板上歌唱，
鞋匠坐在板凳上歌唱，帽匠站着歌唱，
伐木工人唱的歌，農家子在早晨上工、中午休
　　息、太陽西下時唱的歌，
母親的甜潤歌聲，年青的妻子在工作時、少女
　　在縫補或漿洗時的歌聲，
每個人唱着屬於他或她個人而非屬於旁人的歌
　　曲，
白天唱着白天的事情——晚上是成羣的小伙
　　子，健康，友善，
放開喉嚨唱着他們有力度而聲調優美的歌曲。

趙蘿蕤譯

　　惠特曼（1819—1892），生於紐約長島，曾任敎員、排字工人、記者等職。1855年出版詩集《草葉集》（*Leaves of Grass*），最初未獲好評。詩人自1856至1891年間不斷將《草葉集》修改增訂。

80 I Saw in Louisiana a Live-Oak Growing

Walt Whitman

I saw in Louisiana a live-oak growing,
All alone stood it and the moss hung down from the branches,
Without any companion it grew there uttering joyous leaves of dark green,
And its look, rude, unbending, lusty, made me think of myself,
But I wonder'd how it could utter joyous leaves standing alone there without its friend near, for I knew I could not,
And I broke off a twig with a certain number of leaves upon it, and twined around it a little moss,
And brought it away, and have placed it in sight in my room,
It is not needed to remind me as of my own dear friends,
(For I believe lately I think of little else than of them,)
Yet it remains to me a curious token, it makes me think of manly love;
For all that, and though the live-oak glistens there in Louisiana solitary in a wide flat space,
Uttering joyous leaves all its life without a friend a lover near,
I know very well I could not.

八十　在路易斯安那我看見一棵槲樹

瓦爾特・惠特曼

在路易斯安那我看見一棵槲樹生長,
它完全孤獨地站着,苔蘚從枝頭掛下來,
沒有任何同伴,它在那裏生長,發出暗綠色的歡樂的枝葉,
而它的外表粗獷、不屈、强壯,使我想起我自己,
可是我奇怪,孤獨地站在那裏,沒有朋友在近傍的它,怎末能發出歡樂的枝葉,因為我知道這我不能。
我折下它帶有葉子的一枝來,還在上面纏繞些苔蘚,
我把它帶走了,把它放在我眼前,把它放在我房中,
我不需用它來提醒我,我自己親愛的朋友,
(因為我相信最近我想念他們可不少,)
然而它對於我是一個奇異的象徵,它使我想起男子氣概的愛;
儘管如此,儘管這棵槲樹在路易斯安那那兒輝耀,孤獨地站在一個空曠平坦的地方,
一生發出歡樂的枝葉,却沒有一個朋友一個愛人在近傍,
我很知道這我不能。

徐　遲譯

81 O Captain! My Captain!

Walt Whitman

O Captain! my Captain! our fearful trip is done,
The ship has weather'd every rack, the prize we sought is won,
The port is near, the bells I hear, the people all exulting,
While follow eyes the steady keel, the vessel grim and daring;
  But O heart! heart! heart!
    O the bleeding drops of red!
      Where on the deck my Captain lies,
        Fallen cold and dead.

O Captain! my Captain! rise up and hear the bells;
Rise up — for you the flag is flung — for you the bugle trills,
For you bouquets and ribbon'd wreaths — for you the shores crowding,
For you they call, the swaying mass, their eager faces turning;
  Here, Captain! dear father!
    This arm beneath your head;
      It is some dream that on the deck
        You've fallen cold and dead.

My Captain does not answer, his lips are pale and still,
My father does not feel my arm, he has no pulse nor will;
The ship is anchor'd safe and sound, its voyage closed and done;

八十一　啊，船長！我的船長！

瓦爾特·惠特曼

啊，船長！我的船長！可怕的航程已完成；
這船歷盡風險，企求的目標已達成。
港口在望，鐘聲響，人們在歡欣。
千萬雙眼睛注視着船——平穩，勇敢，堅定。
　　但是痛心啊！痛心！痛心！
　　　　瞧一滴滴鮮紅的血！
　　　　　　甲板上躺着我的船長，
　　　　　　　　他倒下去，冰冷，永別。

啊，船長！我的船長！起來吧，傾聽鐘聲；
起來吧，號角為您長鳴，旌旗為您高懸；
迎着您，多少花束花圈——候着您，千万人蜂
　　擁岸邊；
他們向您高呼，擁來擠去，仰起殷切的臉；
　　啊，船長！親愛的父親！
　　　我的手臂托着您的頭！
　　　　　莫非是一場夢：在甲板上
　　　　　　您倒下去，冰冷，永別。

我的船長不作聲，嘴唇慘白，毫不動彈；
我的父親沒感到我的手臂，沒有脈搏，沒有遺
　　言；
船舶拋錨停下，平安抵達；航程終了；

From fearful trip the victor ship comes in with object
  won;
 Exult, O shores! and ring, O bells!
  But I, with mournful tread,
   Walk the deck my Captain lies,
    Fallen cold and dead.

歷經艱險返航，奪得勝利目標。
　　啊，岸上鐘聲齊鳴，啊，人們一片歡騰！
　　但是，我在甲板上，在船長身旁，
　　　心悲切，步履沉重：
　　　　因爲他倒下去，冰冷，永別。

　　　　　　　　　　　　　　　　　楊　霖譯
　　　　　　　　　　　　　　　　　孫　梁校

82 Two Rivulets

Walt Whitman

Two Rivulets side by side,
Two blended, parallel, strolling tides,
Companions, travelers, gossiping as they journey.

For the Eternal Ocean bound,
These ripples, passing surges, streams of Death and Life,
Object and Subject hurrying, whirling by,
The Real and Ideal.

Alternate ebb and flow the Days and Nights,
(Strands of a Trio twining, Present, Future, Past.)

In You, whoe'er you are, my book perusing,
In I myself — in all the World — these ripples flow,
All, all, toward the mystic Ocean tending.

(O yearnful waves! the kisses of your lips!
Your breast so broad, with open arms, O firm, expanded
  shore!)

八十二 雙　溪

瓦爾特·惠特曼

並排的兩條小溪，
兩條混和、平行、漫游的流水，
伴侶、旅客、邊走邊嘮叨。

流向永恒的海洋，
這些微波，順流而過的浪濤，生命和死亡的河
　　流，
主體和客體奔流着，急轉而下，
真實的和理想的。

潮水日日夜夜交替地退了漲、漲了退，
（三股綫絞在一起，現在、未來、過去。）

在你（不管你是誰，凡念我詩的）的心裏，
在我自己的心裏——在全世界的心裏——這些
　　微波流呀流，
一切、一切都流向神秘的海洋。

（啊，叫人懷念的波浪！你的唇上的吻啊！
你的胸脯那麼寬廣，還有你那張開的臂膀，啊，
　　堅實而開闊的海岸啊！）

荒　蕪譯
孫　梁校

83 The Dalliance of the Eagles

Walt Whitman

Skirting the river road, (my forenoon walk, my rest,)
Skyward in air a sudden muffled sound, the dalliance of the eagles,
The rushing amorous contact high in space together,
The clinching interlocking claws, a living, fierce, gyrating wheel,
Four beating wings, two beaks, a swirling mass tight grappling,
In tumbling turning clustering loops, straight downward falling,
Till o'er the river pois'd, the twain yet one, a moment's lull,
A motionless still balance in the air, then parting, talons loosing,
Upward again on slow-firm pinions slanting, their separate diverse flight,
She hers, he his, pursuing.

八十三　鷹的調情

瓦爾特·惠特曼

沿着河邊道路走，（這是我午前的散步、我的
　　休息，）
忽然噗哧一聲冲向天空，鷹兒在調情，
雙雙在太空中，飛快的愛的擁抱，
爪兒交摟，好似生動而迅猛的旋轉車輪，
四扇翅膀撲閃，兩張尖嘴，緊緊攪作一團，
翻來復去打圈圈，直往下降，
一直降到河面上，兩個變成一體，保持暫時平
　　衡，
一動不動，掛在空中，隨後分開，爪兒放鬆，
又各自斜着翅膀向上，緩緩地堅定地各自飛行，
她飛她的，他飛他的——還在追趕。

荒　蕪譯
孫　梁校

84 The Song of the Wage-Slaves

Ernest Jones

The land it is the landlord's,
  The trader's the sea,
The ore the usurer's coffer fills —
  But what remains for me?
The engine whirls for master's craft;
  The steel shines to defend,
With labour's arm, what labour raised,
  For labour's foe to spend.
The camp, the pulpit, and the law
  For rich men's sons are free;
Theirs, theirs the learning, art, and arms —
  But what remains for me?
    The coming hope, the future day,
      When wrong to right shall bow,
    And hearts that have the courage, man,
      To make that future NOW.

I pay for all their learning
  I toil for all their ease;
They render back, in coin for coin;

瓊斯（1819—1869），英國憲章派詩人，1855年出版詩集 *The Battle Day and Other Poems*。憲章運動指1837年倫敦工聯向國會提出普選權等政治要求

八十四　工資奴隸之歌

歐內斯特·瓊斯

地主佔有了土地，
　商人控制了海洋，
礦藏塞滿了掠奪者的錢櫃，
　剩給我的有哪一樣？
機器飛轉，老板如願，
　鋼刀閃亮來作保衛。
勞動者親手創造財富，
　供他們的敵人消費。
法院，兵營，佈道壇，
　公子哥兒隨意盤桓；
學識、藝術、武器，都歸他們，
　留給我的有哪一樣？
　　希望臨近，曙光映現，
　　　不義屈膝在正義面前；
　　心懷義勇的人啊，
　　　快把未來提到今天！

他們讀書，我付學費；
　他們享受，我却勞累。
他們的報酬，每個子兒都精打細算，

的運動，與此運動有關的講演、詩歌、小說和評論文章等稱爲憲章派文學。

> Want, ignorance, disease;
> Toil, toil — and then a cheerless home,
>   Where hungry passions cross;
> Eternal gain to them that give
>   To me eternal loss!
> The hour of leisured happiness
>   The rich alone may see;
> The playful child, the smiling wife —
>   But what remains for me?
>   The coming hope, the future day,
>   When wrong to right shall bow,
>   And hearts that have the courage, man,
>   To make that future NOW.
>
> They render back, those rich men,
>   A pauper's niggard fee,
> Mayhap a prison, — then a grave,
>   And think they are quits with me;
> But not a fond wife's heart that breaks,
>   A poor man's child that dies,
> We score not on our hollow cheeks
>   And in our sunken eyes;
> We read it there, where'er we meet.
>   And as the sun we see,
> Each asks, "The rich have got the earth,
>   And what remains for me?"

——貧困,疾病,愚昧。
幹苦活,幹重活——回家也無歡樂,
　饑火中燒,淚眼相對。
他們永遠有所得,
　我却永遠在受罪。
閑暇的幸福時刻,
　只有富翁能獨享,
還有嬌兒逗樂,嬌妻含笑。
　留給我的有哪一樣?
　　　希望臨近,晨光映現,
　　　　不義屈膝在正義面前;
　　心懷義勇的人啊,
　　　快把未來提到今天!

老財報答的是什麼?
　不過是丟給乞丐的一文錢,
還可能是監牢,——要不是墳墓;
　就這樣他們便認爲結清歸欠。
不算那愛妻的心破碎,
　不算那窮漢的孩子夭折貧賤,
不算我們兩頰瘦削,
　不算我們雙眼深陷。
我們相遇,這些我們一眼看見,
　正如太陽當空出現。
每個都問,"財主吞下了整個地球,
　留給我們的還有哪一件?"

319

> The coming hope, the future day,
>   When wrong to right shall bow,
> And hearts that have the courage, man,
>   To make that future NOW.

We hear the wrong in silence,
  We store it in our brain;
They think us dull, they think us dead,
But we shall rise again:
A trumpet through the lands will ring;
  A heaving through the mass;
A trampling through their palaces
  Until they break like glass:
We'll cease to weep by cherished graves,
  From lonely homes we'll flee;
And still, as rolls our million march,
  Its watchword brave shall be —
> The coming hope, the future day,
>   When wrong to right shall bow,
> And hearts that have the courage, man,
>   To make that future NOW.

　　　　希望臨近，晨光映現，
　　　　　　不義屈膝在正義面前；
　　　　心懷義勇的人啊，
　　　　　　快把未來提到今天！

我們默默的吞聲忍氣，
　　我們把這些在心頭銘記。
他們認為我們獸，認為我們死去；
　　但我們終將重新站起。
號角就要，響遍大地；
　　羣衆將會奮起。
把他們的宮殿踏遍，
　　直到只剩下斷垣殘壁。
我們不再去親人墓旁啜泣，
　　我們將向冷寂的家告辭；
我們百萬大軍邁步前進，
　　英勇戰鬥的口號將是——
　　　　希望臨近，曙光映現，
　　　　　　不義屈膝在正義面前；
　　　　心懷義勇的人啊，
　　　　　　快把未來提到今天！

　　　　　　　　　　　　　孟光裕譯
　　　　　　　　　　　　　孫　梁校

85   Dover Beach

Matthew Arnold

The sea is calm tonight,
The tide is full, the moon lies fair
Upon the straits; on the French coast the light
Gleams and is gone; the cliffs of England stand,
Glimmering and vast, out in the tranquil bay.
Come to the window, sweet is the night-air!
Only, from the long line of spray
Where the sea meets the moon-blanched land.

Listen! you hear the grating roar
Of pebbles which the waves draw back, and fling,
At their return, up the high strand,
Begin, and cease, and then again begin,
With tremulous cadence slow, and bring
The eternal note of sadness in.

Sophocles long ago

阿諾德(1822—1888),英國詩人及文論家,1857年起任牛津大學教授,主講詩學。重要詩篇有《塞西斯》(*Thyrsis*)、《菲洛密拉》(*Philomela*)、《書生——吉布賽人》(*The Scholar—Gypsy*)、《索拉勃與魯斯登》(*Sohrab and Rustum*)等;文藝批評代表作則為兩卷《文藝評論集》(*Essays in Criticism*)。

八十五　多佛海濱[1]

麥修·阿諾德

今晚風平浪靜，
漲潮時，皓月朗照
海峽；彼岸法蘭西，燈影
明滅；此地英倫，懸崖聳峙，
巍然閃現，俯視海灣如鏡。
倚窗兮，夜間清風習習！
惟有浪花蔓延飛濺，
驚濤拍岸，岸上月華如洗。

聽！浪捲卵石訇砰，
狂瀾退，又冲回，翻騰
灘頭，掀起千堆石；
時起，時伏，消長不息，
幽幽咽咽，嫋嫋餘音
萬古愁，不絕如縷。

古人索福克勒斯[2]
———————

　　《多佛海濱》創作於新舊思想交替時期，一方面，傳統的宗教意識和倫理觀念根深蒂固，另方面進化論和不可知論等新學說則方興未艾，令詩人徬徨苦悶。
(1)多佛是英國南方海濱城市。
(2)索福克勒斯（公元前496？－406），古希腊三大悲劇家之一，名著有《安蒂戈尼》等。

Heard it on the Aegean, and it brought
Into his mind the turbid ebb and flow
Of human misery; we
Find also in the sound a thought,
Hearing it by this distant northern sea.

The Sea of Faith
Was once, too, at the full, and round earth's shore
Lay like the folds of a bright girdle furled.
But now I only hear
Its melancholy, long, withdrawing roar,
Retreating, to the breath
Of the night-wind, down the vast edges drear
And naked shingles of the world.

Ah, love, let us be true
To one another! for the world, which seems
To lie before us like a land of dreams,
So various, so beautiful, so new,
Hath really neither joy, nor love, nor light,
Nor certitude, nor peace, nor help for pain;
And we are here as on a darkling plain
Swept with confused alarms of struggle and flight,
Where ignorant armies clash by night.

愛琴海邊聽濤聲,
濁浪滔滔,悠悠哀思:
人間苦難無窮;
千載下,爾我聽濤北海濱,
應有同感油然生。

信仰之海[1]
昔日洶湧澎湃,
波光似錦帶,繚繞寰球。
如今衰朽,
只聽得濤音淒惻,
退潮時奄奄一息,
夜風嗚咽,荒灘漫無際,
浪去也,席捲平沙頑石。

眷戀莫背棄!
眼前紅塵迷離,
依稀似幻夢:
新奇、瑰麗、絢爛多姿,
其實無愛,無光,無生趣,
不安,不寧,苦海伶仃;
彷彿荒原陰森,
黑夜裏烏合之衆交鋒,
亂紛紛相爭,惶惶然逃遁。

孫　梁譯

---

[1]指宗教信仰。

86 Memorial Verses (Extract)

Matthew Arnold

Goethe in Weimar sleeps, and Greece,
Long since, saw Byron's struggle cease.
But one such death remain'd to come.
The last poetic verse is dumb —
We stand to-day by Wordsworth's tomb.
When Byron's eyes were shut in death,
We bowed our head and held our breath.
He taught us little; but our soul
Had *felt* him like the thunder's roll.
With shivering heart the strife we saw
Of passion with eternal law;
And yet with reverential awe
We watch'd the fount of fiery life
Which serv'd for that Titanic strife.

When Goethe's death was told, we said:
Sunk, then, is Europe's sagest head.
Physician of the iron age
Goethe has done his pilgrimage.
He took the suffering human race,
He read each wound, each weakness clear;
And struck his finger on the place,
And said — *Thou ailest here, and here!*
He look'd on Europe's dying hour
Of fitful dream and feverish power;

阿諾德在《悼詩》中沉痛而眞摯地悼念歌德、拜倫與沃茲沃斯。

(1)指魏瑪,德國東部城市;十八世紀屬薩克遜——魏

八十六 悼 詩（節選）

麥修·阿諾德

歌德棄人世，長眠在魏城。(1)
希臘人懷念，拜倫曠世英。
死神幾曾惜，人間攝詩魂。
今朝又吊唁，沃茲沃斯靈。
吁嗟乎詩翁，喑啞竟無聲。
拜倫雙目瞑，舉世哀以敬。
敎誨雖無多，心受雷電震。
驚心又動魄，感觸不能已：
遵循永恒則，激情盪胸臆。
吾儕敬畏深，觀此心火紅，
心為情之源，爭鬥魄力雄！

憶昔噩耗傳：歌德忽長殂，
俱云歐洲厄，哲人喪其魂；
濁世為良醫，歷盡生之程。
胸懷容衆生，診治諸病症。
斷然指癥結，明言此毒根！
慧眼視末世：夢囈和權迷；
預感歐羅巴，已罹不治症。

瑪公國。歌德於1775年應魏瑪公爵之約，抵達該地。此後數十年內，參與政務，襄助建設，研究科學，進行創作，並薦舉人才，直至逝世。

His eye plunged down the weltering strife,
The turmoil of expiring life —
He said: *The end is everywhere,*
Art still has truth, take refuge there!
And he was happy, if to know
Causes of things, and far below
His feet to see the lurid flow
Of terror, and insane distress,
And headlong fate, be happiness.

And Wordsworth! — Ah, pale ghosts, rejoice!
For never has such soothing voice
Been to your shadowy world convey'd,
Since erst, at morn, some wandering shade
Heard the clear song of Orpheus come
Through Hades, and the mournful gloom.
Wordsworth is gone from us — and ye,
Ah, may ye feel his voice as we!
He too upon a wintry clime
Had fallen — on this iron time
Of doubts, disputes, distractions, fears.
He found us when the age had bound
Our souls in its benumbing round;
He spoke, and loosed our hearts in tears.

擾攘無止境，生命之火隱──
大千臨末日，惟有藝術眞！
紅塵諸恐怖，險峻諸命運，
瘋狂與災難，一一察其因；
如斯究本源，幸福即化身。

沃茲沃斯逝，羣鬼應慶幸！
緣此慰安曲，從未吟幽冥；
徐非奧菲斯(1)，樂聲殊清新，
拂曉幽靈聽，光明地獄臨。
詩翁雖長逝，歌聲感人深！
寒冬何嚴酷，恐怖與紛爭，
迷惑又紊亂，此際詩人隕。
時代磨靈魂，桎梏拘人心；
一旦詩翁吟，洒淚洗愁根。

蘇仲翔譯
孫　梁校

---

(1)奧菲斯爲希腊神話中詩人，擅音樂，其樂聲能感動頑石。

87 Three Shadows

Dante Gabriel Rossetti

I looked and saw your eyes
   In the shadow of your hair
As a traveller sees the stream
   In the shadow of the wood;
And I said, "My faint heart sighs
   Ah me! to linger there,
To drink deep and to dream
   In that sweet solitude."

I looked and saw your heart
   In the shadow of your eyes,
As a seeker sees the gold
   In the shadow of the stream;
And I said, "Ah me! what art
   Should win the immortal prize,
Whose want must make life cold
   And Heaven a hollow dream?"

I looked and saw your love
   In the shadow of your heart,
As a diver sees the pearl
   In the shadow of the sea;
And I murmured, not above
   My breath, but all apart, —
"Ah! you can love, true girl,
   And is your love for me?"

但丁‧羅賽蒂(1828—1882),英國詩人及畫家,父親原藉意大利。曾組成"先拉斐爾派兄弟會"(Pre-Raphaelite Brotherhood),主張回到意大利文藝復興拉斐爾以前的藝術傳統。1870年出版《羅賽蒂詩

八十七　三重影

但丁·加百列爾·羅賽蒂

在你秀髮的陰影中我看見你的眼睛,
　　彷彿旅行者在樹木的陰影中看見溪流清清;
我說,"哎!我柔弱的心兒呻吟,要駐停,
　　並在那甜蜜的寂靜中暢飲,沉入夢境。"

在你眼睛的陰影中我看見你的心靈,
　　彷彿淘金者在溪流的陰影中看見燦燦黃金;
我說,"哎!憑什麼技藝才能贏得這不朽的獎品?
　　缺少它,必定使生命寒冷,天堂如夢般淒清。"

在你心靈的陰影中我看見你的愛情,
　　彷彿潛水者在海水的陰影中看見珍珠瑩瑩;
我喃喃絮語,並不高聲,還遠離着一程,——
　　"啊!真心的姑娘,你能愛,但能愛我不能?"

吳鈞陶譯

集》,1881年出版詩集《歌謠與十四行詩》(*Ballads and Sonnets*),其中包括十四行詩組《生命之逆旅》(*House of Life*)。

88　A Pause

Christina Georgina Rossetti

They made the chamber sweet with flowers and leaves,
　　And the bed sweet with flowers on which I lay;
　　While my soul, love-bound, loitered on its way.
I did not hear the birds about the eaves,
Nor hear the reapers talk among the sheaves:
　　Only my soul kept watch from day to day,
　　My thirsty soul kept watch for one away: —
Perhaps he loves, I thought, remembers, grieves,
At length there came the step upon the stair,
　　Upon the lock the old familiar hand:
Then first my spirit seemed to scent the air
　　Of Paradise; then first the tardy sand
Of time ran golden; and I felt my hair
　　Put on a glory, and my soul expand.

　　克里斯蒂娜・羅賽蒂（1830—1894），但丁・羅賽蒂的妹妹，1847年出版第一部作品《詩選》(*Verses*)，1862年發表長詩《精靈市場》(*Goblin Market*)。其他作品有《王子歷程等詩集》(*The Prince's Progress*

八十八 逗 留

克里斯蒂娜·喬金娜·羅賽蒂

用鮮花和綠葉他們使室內芬芳,
　馥郁的花香撒滿我安息的臥床;
　我的靈魂追隨着愛的踪迹,四處飄蕩。
我從不聞屋檐下鳥兒細語呢喃,
也不聞穀堆邊收割人談笑風生;
　唯有我的靈魂每日在守望,
　我飢渴的靈魂把別離的人兒盼望:——
我想,也許他愛我,懷念我,爲我悲傷。
終於從階梯上傳來了脚步聲響,
　門把上又重見那以往熟悉的手:
頓時我的心靈彷彿感到天堂的氣息
　在空中蕩漾;那遲緩的流沙——
時光也閃現金色;我感到一輪光暈
　在我髮間輝耀,我的靈魂升華。

虞蘇美譯

孫　梁校

---

and Other Poems)、《詩集》(Poems)、《新詩集》
(New Poems)等。
　《逗留》描寫一個女郎死後,靈魂依然徘徊着,
等待遠方的愛人來臨。

89 When I Am Dead, My Dearest

Christina Georgina Rossetti

When I am dead, my dearest,
   Sing no sad songs for me;
Plant thou no roses at my head,
   Nor shady cypress tree:
Be the green grass above me
   With showers and dewdrops wet:
And if thou wilt, remember,
   And if thou wilt, forget.

I shall not see the shadows,
   I shall not feel the rain;
I shall not hear the nightingale
   Sing on as if in pain:
And dreaming through the twilight
   That doth not rise nor set,
Haply I may remember,
   And haply may forget.

八十九 當我離開人間,最親愛的
克里斯蒂娜·喬金娜·羅賽蒂

當我離開人間,最親愛的,
　別為我哀歌悲切;
我的墓前不要栽玫瑰,
　也不要柏樹茂密;
願綠茵覆蓋我的身軀,
　沾着濕潤的靈珠雨水;
假如你願意,就把我懷念,
　假如你願意,就把我忘却。

我不會重見那蔭影,
　不會感覺雨天來臨;
我不會聽見那夜鶯
　一聲聲彷彿哀鳴;
我置身夢境,在朦朧的黎明,
　它從不升起,也永不沉淪;
也許我會懷念,
　也許我會忘却。

虞蘇美譯

孫　梁校

《當我離開人間,最親愛的》表現詩人對死亡的探索以及對友情的依戀。

90 Little Stone

Emily Dickinson

How happy is the little Stone
That rambles in the Road alone,
And doesn't care about Careers
And Exigencies never fears —
Whose Coat of elemental Brown
A passing Universe put on,
And independent as the Sun
Associates or glows alone,
Fulfilling absolute Decree
In casual simplicity —

九十　小石

艾米莉·狄更遜

這顆小石何等幸福,
獨自在路旁漫步。
它不汲汲於功名,
也從不爲變故擔心。
變幻的宇宙也得披
它質樸的棕色外衣;
它獨立不羈如太陽,
與衆輝映,或獨自閃光。
它順應天意,
單純,一味自然。

汪義羣譯

孫　梁校

狄更遜(1830—1886),生於美國馬薩諸塞州,家境富裕,終身未嫁。自1862年起足不出戶,甚至拒絕最親近的朋友來訪。一生共寫了一千八百首詩,詩稿死後才被發現,陸續出版。

91 Presentiment

Emily Dickinson

Presentiment — is that long Shadow— on the Lawn —
Indicative that Suns go down —

The Notice to the startled Grass
That Darkness — is about to pass —

九十一　預感

艾米莉·狄更遜

預感——是草坪上——長曳的陰影——
暗示着夕陽西沉——

啓示驚惶的青草
黑暗——行將籠罩——

　　　　　　　　　　　　　汪義羣譯

　　　　　　　　　　　　　孫　梁校

92 I'm Nobody

Emily Dickinson

I'm nobody, who are you?
Are you nobody too?
Then there's a pair of us.
Don't tell — they'd banish us, you know.

How dreary to be somebody,
How public — like a frog —
To tell your name the livelong June
To an admiring bog.

九十二　我是無名之輩

艾米莉·狄更遜

我是無名之輩，你是誰？
你也是無名之輩？
那麼，咱倆是一對——且莫聲張！
你懂嘛，他們容不得咱倆。

做個名人多無聊！
像青蛙——到處招搖——
向一窪仰慕的泥塘
把自己的大名整天宣揚！

汪義羣譯

孫　梁校

93 A Match

Algernon Charles Swinburne

If love were what the rose is,
    And I were like the leaf,
Our lives would grow together
In sad or singing weather,
Blown fields or flowerful closes,
    Green pleasure or grey grief;
If love were what the rose is,
    And I were like the leaf.

If I were what the words are,
    And love were like the tune,
With double sound and single
Delight our lips would mingle,
With kisses glad as birds are
    That get sweet rain at noon;
If I were what the words are,
    And love were like the tune.

If you were life, my darling,

斯溫本（1837—1909），生於倫敦，先在法國受教育，後進牛津大學。1865年發表詩劇《開來敦的阿塔蘭塔》（*Atalanta in Calydon*），次年出版《詩篇與歌謠》（*Poems and Ballads*）。其他主要詩作有

九十三 配 偶

阿爾杰農・查爾斯・斯溫本

如果愛情好似香艷的玫瑰,
　　而我好似它的葉片青翠,
我們的生命將在一起生長,
無論天氣陰沉或晴朗,
處在豐饒的原野或花徑,
　　感受綠色的歡樂或灰色的苦悶;
如果愛情好似香艷的玫瑰,
　　而我好似它的葉片青翠。

如果我好似密語甜言,
　　而愛情好似曲調綿綿,
我們的嘴將一同歌唱,
兩種嗓音,但是一種歡暢,
欣悅的親吻彷彿飛鳥
　　在中午得到甘露淋澆;
如果我好似蜜語甜言,
　　而愛情好似曲調綿綿。

如果愛情好似生命,我的親人,

《黎明前的詩歌》(*Songs before Sunrise*)、三部曲:《查斯特拉德》(*Chastelard*)、《波士威爾》(*Bothwell*)、《瑪麗・斯圖亞特》(*Mary Stuart*)。

    And I your love were death,
We'd shine and snow together
Ere March made sweet the weather
With daffodil and starling
    And hours of fruitful breath;
If you were life, my darling,
    And I your love were death.

If you were thrall to sorrow,
    And I were page to joy,
We'd play for lives and seasons
With loving looks and treasons
And tears of night and morrow
    And laughs of maid and boy;
If you were thrall to sorrow,
    And I were page to joy.

If you were April's lady,
    And I were lord in May,
We'd throw with leaves for hours
And draw for days with flowers,
Till day like night were shady
    And night were bright like day;
If you were April's lady,
    And I were lord in May.

而我,你的愛人,好似死神,
我們將一起歡笑,一起沮喪,
直等到三月使天青氣爽,
帶着水仙的芬芳,椋鳥的鳴囀,
　　和散發豐收氣息的時光;
如果愛情好似生命,我的親人,
　　而我,你的愛人,好似死神。

如果你好似被憂愁束縛的奴隸,
　　而我好似受歡樂差遣的僕役,
我們將一生一世,一年四季,
脈脈含情,又作負心的遊戲,
晚也哭,朝也哭,淚水潸潸,
　　像女孩,像男孩,笑聲朗朗;
如果你好似被憂愁束縛的奴隸,
　　而我好似受歡樂差遣的僕役。

如果你好似四月的貴婦,
　　而我好似五月的貴人,
我們將一小時一小時把葉子拋擲,
又一天天地用鮮花作畫,
直到白天像黑夜一樣陰暗,
　　黑夜像白天一樣明亮;
如果你好似四月的貴婦,
　　而我好似五月的貴人。

If you were queen of pleasure,
   And I were king of pain,
We'd hunt down love together,
Pluck out his flying feather,
And teach his feet a measure,
   And find his mouth a rein;
If you were queen of pleasure,
   And I were king of pain.

如果你好似歡樂的皇后,
　　而我好似痛苦的帝胄,
我們將一同去追捕愛情,
把它飄揚的羽毛拔淨,
教它的雙腳循規蹈矩,
　　將它的嘴套上拶具;
如果你好似歡樂的皇后,
　　而我好似痛苦的帝胄。

　　　　　　　　　　吳鈞陶譯

94 Love at Sea

Imitated from Théophile Gautier

Algernon Charles Swinburne

We are in love's land to-day;
    Where shall we go?
Love, shall we start or stay,
    Or sail or row?
There's many a wind and way,
And never a May but May;
We are in love's hand to-day;
    Where shall we go?

Our land-wind is the breath
Of sorrows kissed to death
   And joys that were;
Our ballast is a rose;
Our way lies where God knows
   And love knows where.
     We are in love's hand to-day —

Our seamen are fledged Loves,

九十四　海上的愛情
仿泰奧菲爾·戈蒂耶⑴詩作

阿爾杰農·查爾斯·斯溫本

我們今天正在愛情的陸上，
　　我們將要去何方？
愛人，是逗留還是啓航？
　　是揚帆還是划槳？
有許多路，有許多風吹蕩，
但只有五月才是五月的春光；
今天我們正在愛情的手上；
　　我們將要去何方？

我們陸上的風是憂愁的呼吸，
這憂愁被親吻吻得奄奄一息，
　　又是那過去的欣喜；
我們用一株玫瑰壓在艙底；
我們的路伸展着，上帝
　　和愛情知道它在哪裏。
　　　今天我們正在愛情的手上——

我們的水手是羽毛豐滿的愛神，

⑴戈蒂耶（1811—1872），法國詩人、小說家兼評論家。他的詩歌追求"造型美"，主張"爲藝術而藝術"。

Our masts are bills of doves,
   Our decks fine gold;
Our ropes are dead maids' hair,
Our stores are love-shafts fair
   And manifold.
      We are in love's land to-day —

Where shall we land you, sweet?
On fields of strange men's feet,
   Or fields near home?
Or where the fire-flowers blow,
Or where the flowers of snow
   Or flowers of foam?
      We are in love's hand to-day —

Land me, she says, where love
Shows but one shaft, one dove,
   One heart, one hand.
— A shore like that, my dear,
Lies where no man will steer,
   No maiden land.

我們的桅杆是斑鳩的尖喙長伸，
　　　　我們的甲板用純金製成；
　　死去的少女的金髮是我們的纜繩；
　　愛神的利箭是我們的補給用品，
　　　　是形形色色的貯存。
　　　　　　今天我們正在愛情的陸上——

　　愛人，我們在哪兒送你上岸？
　　是在踩着陌生人腳印的土壤，
　　　　還是在靠近家屋的田園？
　　還是在那兒火之花熊熊怒放，
　　還是在那兒雪之花紛紛開綻，
　　　　還是浪之花陣陣飛濺？
　　　　　　今天我們正在愛情的手上——

　　她說，送我到那兒由愛情駐守，
　　它只有一根利箭，一隻斑鳩，
　　　　一顆心，一隻手。
　　——親愛的，像這樣的港口，
　　沒有青年男子將向那兒駕舟，
　　　　沒有少女登上灘頭。

　　　　　　　　　　　　吳鈞陶譯

95 Reveille

Alfred Edward Houseman

Wake: the silver dusk returning
   Up the beach of darkness brims,
And the ship of sunrise burning
   Strands upon the eastern rims.

Wake: the vaulted shadow shatters,
   Trampled to the floor it spanned,
And the tent of night in tatters
   Straws the sky-pavilioned land.

Up, lad, up, 'tis late for lying:
   Hear the drums of morning play;
Hark, the empty highways crying
   "Who'll beyond the hills away?"

Towns and countries woo together,
   Forelands beacon, belfries call;
Never lad that trod on leather
   Lived to feast his heart with all.

Up, lad; thews that lie and cumber

霍思曼（1859—1936），生於英國渥斯特郡，歷任牛津、劍橋大學拉丁文教授。1896年出版《西羅普郡少年》（*Shropshire Lad*），1922年發表第二本詩

九十五　起身號

阿爾弗萊德‧愛德華‧霍思曼

醒醒：銀灰的暝色回來了，
　　　漫上茫茫黑暗的海邊；
朝日的船舶通紅的燒着，
　　　遠遠擱淺在東方邊緣。

醒醒：穹窿的樓頂踏破了，
　　　廢基上堆起碎影重重；
夜天的營幕裂成片片，
　　　倒在大地上散亂縱橫。

起來，孩子，再不能睡了：
　　　你聽清晨的鼓聲在奏；
聽呀，空蕩的大道叫喚着
　　　"趕往山外的有哪一個？"

鄉間和鎮上一齊在敦促，
　　　前方起烽火，鐘樓正召集；
從來腳穿皮靴的男兒
　　　在世上沒有能享受一切。

起來，孩子，肌肉盡盤蜷

集《詩後集》(*Last Poems*)，死後出版《詩外集》(*More Poems*)。

Sunlit pallets never thrive;
Morns abed and daylight slumber
　　　Were not meant for man alive.

Clay lies still, but blood's a rover;
　　　Breath's a ware that will not keep.
Up, lad: when the journey's over
　　　There'll be time enough to sleep.

陽光的藁薦，決不會榮茂；
早晨賴床，白天裏酣睡，
　　不是活的人份內所應做。

泥土不動，但血液是遊子；
　　呼吸是用不了多久的爐灶。
起來，孩子，待旅程完畢時，
　　你盡有時間睡你的覺。

周煦良譯

96 Bring, in This Timeless Grave to Throw

Alfred Edward Houseman

    Bring in this timeless grave to throw,
No cypress, sombre on the snow;
Snap not from the bitter yew
His leaves that live December through;
Break no rosemary, bright with rime
And sparkling to the cruel clime;
Nor plod the winter land to look
For willows in the icy brook
To cast them leafless round him: bring
No spray that ever buds in spring.

    But if the Christmas field has kept
Awns the last gleaner overstept,
Or shrivelled flax, whose flower is blue
A single season, never two;
Or if one haulm whose year is o'er
Shivers on the upland frore,
— Oh, bring from hill and stream and plain
Whatever will not flower again,
To give him comfort: he and those

---

(1) 柏樹在希臘與羅馬俱被視爲死的象徵。

(2) 據稱杉葉有毒,牛馬不可食。

(3) 迷迭香用於葬儀中。

九十六　雪中莫去折黯淡的柏枝

阿爾弗萊德‧愛德華‧霍思曼

雪中莫去折黯淡的柏枝(1)
投入此墓中,杳杳無歲時;
莫去折味苦有毒的杉樹(2),
杉葉能將十二月捱渡;
莫採迷迭香(3),瞪瞪着濃霜,
在凜冽寒氣中閃映冬陽;
也莫要跋涉歲暮的原郊,
冰溪中尋找衰柳的空條(4)
將來環繞他身側;莫擷
任何歲寒枝,春來還發葉。

　　但如果冬節的田野猶存
往日拾穗者踏過的麥莖;
或是一些乾萎的胡麻,
青花只開一夏,不再發;
或一根豆梗,其時節已畢,
留在凍結的高地中顫慄──
啊,不管從原野,山邊或水隈,
把一切不再開花的載來
給他以慰藉,當他潛進那

---

(4) 英國古民歌中似以柳象徵愁恨,見莎劇《奧賽羅》
第四幕第三景之歌。

Shall bide eternal bedfellows
Where low upon the couch he lies
Whence he never shall arise.

他從此不能升起的泉下,
這些將留着和他作陪,
千年,萬年,一榻兒沉睡。

                                    周煦良譯

97 When I Came Last to Ludlow

Alfred Edward Houseman

When I came last to Ludlow
   Amidst the moonlight pale,
Two friends kept step beside me,
   Two honest lads and hale.

Now Dick lies long in the churchyard,
   And Ned lies long in jail,
And I come home to Ludlow
   Amidst the moonlight pale.

九十七 上次我囘到祿如鎭

阿爾弗萊德・愛德華・霍思曼

上次我囘到祿如鎭，
　　一路上戴着淡月，
跟我走有兩個小朋友，
　　兩個都天眞而活躍。

狄克呢，已長睡墓園裏，
　　奈德是久困於縲絏，
我今祿如鎭又歸來，
　　一路戴着淡月。

周煦良譯

98 Hughley Steeple

Alfred Edward Houseman

The vane on Hughley steeple
  Veers bright, a far-known sign,
And there lie Hughley people,
  And there lie friends of mine.
Tall in their midst the tower
  Divides the shade and sun,
And the clock strikes the hour
  and tells the time to none.

To south the headstones cluster,
  The sunny mounds lie thick;
The dead are more in muster
  At Hughley than the quick.
North, for a soon-told number,
  Chill graves the sexton delves,
And steeple-shadowed slumber
  The slayers of themselves.

To north, to south, lie parted,
  With Hughley tower above,
The kind, the single-hearted,
  The lads I used to love.
And, south or north, 'tis only

九十八　休來寺

阿爾弗萊德・愛德華・霍思曼

風標鏾鏾的轉動着，
　　　遠望見休來的鐘樓，
那裏長眠着休來人，
　　　那裏長眠着我朋友。
休來高立在當中，
　　　隔離開陽光與陰影，
鐘樓朝夕報時辰，
　　　悠悠的永無人省。

南面的石表密成林，
　　　陽光下壘壘崇墓；
在休來死者要多於
　　　檢閱時生者的人數。
北面，爲一般夭折者
　　　有寺工築下的冷墳，
而沉沉樓影酣睡的
　　　是些自殺掉的人。

在南面北面分隔着，
　　　有休來寺高臨其間，
那艮善的，我往昔篤愛的，
　　　心地樸實的少年。
而無論南面或北面，

A choice of friends one knows,
And I shall ne'er be lonely
    Asleep with these or those.

好朋友只得幾個,
而我是永不會孤單的,
　　和這些或那些同臥。

　　　　　　　　周煦良譯

99 The Pond

Edward Thomas

Bright clouds of may
Shade half the pond.
Beyond,
All but one bay
Of emerald
Tall reeds
Like criss-cross bayonets
Where a bird once called,
Lies bright as the sun.
No one heeds.
The light wind frets
And drifts the scum
Of may-blossom.
Till the moorhen calls
Again
Naught's to be done
By birds or men.
Still the may falls.

托馬斯（1878—1917），出生於倫敦，早期詩文跟斯賓塞、馬羅等田園詩一脈相承。結識美國詩人羅伯特・弗洛斯特(Robert Frost)後，詩風轉爲凝鍊。

九十九 池

愛德華·托馬斯

五月明麗的行雲
浮影半掩池塘。
遠方,
惟海灣綠碧
璀璨如艷陽;
纖長的蘆葦
彷彿刺刀交錯
曾記否?有鳥兒啾囀。
無人理會。
微風吹拂
五月鮮花蓓蕾
落英繽紛。
紅松鷄啼叫
二遍
春易老
無可奈何人與鳥。
五月悄悄去了。

宗 白譯

第一次世界大戰爆發後應徵入伍,在法國東北戰場犧牲。作品有 *The South County*,*Light and Twilight*,*The Happy-Go-Lucky Morgans* 等。

100 July

Edward Thomas

Naught moves but clouds, and in the glassy lake
Their doubles and the shadow of my boat.
The boat itself stirs only when I break
This drowse of heat and solitude afloat
To prove if what I see be bird or mote,
Or learn if yet the shore woods be awake.

Long hours since dawn grew, — spread, — and passed on high
And deep below, — I have watched the cool reeds hung
Over images more cool in imaged sky:
Nothing there was worth thinking of so long;
All that the ring-doves say, far leaves among,
Brims my mind with content thus still to lie.

一〇〇 七月

愛德華・托馬斯

萬物寧謐，惟有流雲，晶瑩的湖泊，
雲影緩移，浮泛着舟影。
扁舟輕蕩，我用槳兒划破
沉沉的炎熱，和迷離的寂寞，
爲了辨認：望見的是鳥抑或纖塵，
爲了探明：湖畔樹林是否蘇醒。

晨曦早已微明──瀰漫──飄向晴空
又溶於碧波；我久久凝視泠泠的蘆葦
影入雲天氄氄的水中，涼意更濃；
在這悠悠的時光，物我兩忘
遠處樹叢，斑尾鴿喁喁細語，
我靜臥諦聽，恍惚置身仙境。

宗　白譯

Bibliography

M. H. Abrams (gen. ed.), et al., *The Norton Anthology of English Literature,* Vol. I, Parts 1, 2; Vol. II, Parts 1, 2, 3 (New York, London: W. W. Norton, 1979, 1974).

Matthew Arnold, *Essays Literary and Critical* (London: J. M. Dent and Sons, 1911).

Matthew Arnold (ed.), *Poems of Wordsworth* (London: Macmillan, 1919).

Lord Byron, *Poems,* Vols. 1, 2, 3 (London: J. M. Dent and Sons, 1948).

M. V. Doren, *Walt Whitman* (New York: The Viking Press, 1945).

T. S. Eliot, *Collected Poems* (New York: Harcourt, Brace, 1936).

Allen Freer and John Andrew (co-ed.), *The Cambridge Book of English Verse* (Cambridge: The Univ. Press, 1976).

Helen Gardner (ed.), *The Metaphysical Poets* (Middlesex: Penguin Books, 1968).

Lord Gorell, *John Keats: The Principle of Beauty* (London: Sylvan Press, 1948).

Stephen Graham (ed.), *100 Best Poems in the English Language* (London: Ernest Benn, 1952).

John Hayward (ed.), *The Penguin Book of English Verse* (Middlesex: Penguin Books, 1956).

Lafcadio Hearn, *On Poets* (Tokyo: Hokuseido, 1934).

Philip Hobsbaum, *Tradition and Experiment in English Poetry* (London: Macmillan, 1979).

A. E. Houseman, *A Shropshire Lad* (Philadelphia, David McKay, 1950).

E. D. Jones (ed.), *English Critical Essays: Nineteenth Century* (Oxford Univ. Press, 1932, 1929).

M. A. Keeling (ed.), *Poems of Nature and Romance* (Oxford Univ. Press, 1923).

Liu Wu-chi and Irving Yucheng Lo (co-ed.), *Sunflower Splendor* (New York: Anchor Press/Doubleday, 1975).

F. T. Palgrave and C. D. Lewis (co-ed.), *The Golden Treasury* (London and Glasgow: Collins, 1980, 1954).

Ezra Pound (ed.), *Active Poetry* (London: Faber and Faber, 1938).

Sir Arthur Quiller-Couch (ed.), *The Oxford Book of English Verse* (Oxford Univ. Press, 1943, 1939).

W.H.D. Rouse (ed.), *Milton's Poetical Works* (London and Toronto: J. M. Dent and Sons, 1929).

Mark Schorer, et al. (eds.), *Criticism: The Foundations of Modern Literary Judgment* (New York: Harcourt, Brace, 1948).

William Shakespeare, *Shakespeare's Sonnets* (London: George G. Harrap, 1925).

Louis Untermeyer (ed.), *A Treasury of Great Poems: English and American* (New York: Simon and Schuster, 1942).

Oscar Williams (ed.), *Master Poems of the English Language* (New York: Washington Square Press, 1967).

William Wordsworth, *The Poetical Works of Wordsworth* (Oxford Univ. Press, 1940).

參考書目

《喬叟文集》,方重譯;上海文藝出版社,1962年;上海譯文出版社,1979年。

《莎士比亞全集》,第十一卷:(選錄)《十四行詩》,梁宗岱譯;北京,人民文學出版社,1978年。

《莎士比亞評論滙編》,楊周翰編選:(選錄)瓊生《題莎士比亞遺著》,卞之琳譯;北京,中國社會科學出版社,1979年。

《世界著名作家詩歌選》,李采靡編選:(選錄)卞之琳譯莎士比亞十四行詩,殷寶書譯彌爾頓詩;香港,上海書局,1977年。

《復樂園·鬥士參孫·短詩選》,彌爾頓著,朱維之譯;上海譯文出版社,1981年。

《英詩譯稿》,郭沫若譯;上海譯文出版社,1981年。

《沫若譯詩集》;上海,新文藝出版社,1954年。

《布萊克詩選》,袁可嘉等譯;人民文學出版社,1957年。

《彭斯詩選》,王佐良譯;人民文學出版社,1959年。

《英國詩文選譯集》,王佐良譯;北京,外語教學與研究出版社,1980年。

《番石榴集》,朱湘選譯:(選錄)《老舟子行》;上海,商務印書館,1935年。

《拜倫詩選》,查良錚譯;上海譯文出版社,1982年。

《雪萊抒情詩選》,查良錚譯;人民文學出版社,1982年。

《濟慈詩選》,查良錚譯;人民文學出版社,1958年。

《英國憲章派詩選》,袁可嘉譯;上海文藝出版社,1960年。

《魯拜集》,莪默·伽亞謨著,愛德華·菲茲吉拉德英譯,郭沫若譯;人民文學出版社,1958年。

《聞一多全集》,第三卷,朱自清、郭沫若等編:(選錄)《白朗寧夫人的情詩(一)》;上海,開明書店,1948年。

《抒情十四行詩集》,白朗寧夫人著,方平譯;上海,新文藝出版社,1956年;四川人民出版社,1982年。

《國外作品選譯》,第八期:(選錄)荒蕪譯惠特曼詩;外文出版局《編譯參考》編輯部編印,1979年。

《譯文》,茅盾主編,1954年6月號:(選錄)卞之琳譯拜倫詩;北京,人民文學出版社。

同上,1955年9月號:(選錄)徐遲譯惠特曼詩。

《美國文學叢刊》,1983年第1期:(選錄)趙葳莚譯惠特曼詩;全國美國文學研究會編;山東人民出版社。